1 - 25 - 96

MW00780570

GROWING THROUGH GRIEF

GROWING THROUGH GRIEF

Bill Flatt

Christian Communications
P.O. Box 150
Nashville, TN 37202

Growing Through Grief

Copyrighted © 1987 by Gospel Advocate Co.
Second Printing, 1989

All rights reserved. No part of this publication may be reproduced, stored in a
retrieval system, or transmitted in any form or by any means without the prior
permission of the publisher.

Published by Christian Communications
A Division of Gospel Advocate Co.
P.O. Box 150, Nashville, TN 37202

ISBN 0-89225-305-3

I respectfully and affectionately dedicate this book to:

Katherine Hinds-Smythe
Jack Redden
Mora Crosthwait

and to all the widows and widowers of our Grief Recovery
of Widowed groups.

CONTENTS

A Special Note: For stylistic reasons, the pronoun "he" is sometimes used in this book in a generic sense referring to both sexes. In doing so, the author intends no bias toward women.

PREFACE

A decade ago, a friend and student of mine, Jack Redden, and I were invited to participate in a program on death and dying sponsored by the University of Tennessee. During this program, we had an opportunity to visit and to talk about ways of helping people who are grieving because of the loss of loved ones. Also during that time, Jack, who is executive vice president of Memphis Memorial Funeral Home and Park, asked me if I could devise a group counseling approach for the purpose of helping people deal with grief. I was glad to accept this challenge, since I had used a group method for counseling in general and also for counseling divorced people. I thought it would be ideal as a method for helping widows and widowers work through grief. That judgment has proved to be accurate.

During the years since that program, more than five hundred widows and widowers have gone through one of these grief therapy groups. The groups meet two hours a week for six weeks. Each meeting is somewhat structured so that we are sure to cover certain topics, yet loosely enough organized to allow for discussion of whatever is on the hearts of the participants.

The group method is especially helpful in dealing with grief. It brings together people who have similar concerns. Thus, they find it easy to be interested in what others say, and they also find it natural to reinforce, to be empathetic, and to try to help others in the group. Without a single exception, each person who has been in these groups has been very ready to listen and to assist others. The participants know what it's like to grieve. They share information with each other that is often extremely helpful.

From the beginning, a measurement has been taken before and after each group. Jack was a counseling student of mine at that time at the Harding Graduate School of Religion and was working on a guided research paper dealing with grief. He took "The Grief Recovery of Widowed" as the topic for his paper. This necessitated his sitting in on the first six or so groups that I led at the Park. He and other personnel at the cemetery (especially Mora Crosthwait) were extremely helpful gathering the groups together, preparing a place for the meetings, providing refreshments, and even transporting widows and widowers who had difficulty getting there.

After Jack finished his paper, we continued to do the groups. Jack has done a number of groups on his own, I have continued to do some groups, and others have helped as well. We have continued to measure grief in various ways, both before and after the group meets. We have thus collected perhaps more data on grieving widows and widowers than has ever been collected before. It's primarily through these group counseling meetings, as well as through individual sessions with these courageous widows and widowers through the years, that I've gleaned the insights offered in this book. Those folks know much about grieving and what helps one in grief work, because they've been there.

As you read, always remember that no two people are exactly alike, that no two people will go through quite the same experiences during grief, and that no two people settle grief in exactly the same way. Also, read with appreciation of these widows and widowers who are sharing their hearts with you. Their wish and mine is for you to be able to work through *your* grief and to be able to help others also work through theirs.

Bill Flatt
Memphis, Tennessee

1

A PERSONAL STORY

Not long ago, I went to the funeral of a person who was related to a friend of mine. She was an older woman whom I knew only casually. I was at the funeral primarily because of my friend. Normally, I wouldn't think of such a funeral as being a major challenge for me. However, during this funeral I found myself with tears in my eyes several times.

One of the most trying times for me was when the minister was addressing the children. He said to them, "When you go by the casket of your mom, say, 'Thank you, Mom, for all you've done for us. Thank you, Mom, for what you were.' " That was a real challenge for me, because I had lost my own mom about nine months earlier. The memory of that was still on my heart. And when the minister said those words, I was applying them to my mom. I was telling her again how much she meant to me and how I appreciated her.

Grief is like that. We think we've worked through it, but it's still there to some extent. Memories are stored in our minds. They are intellectual. They are emotional. They are very real.

Grief is very difficult to understand. I remember when my mom neared death. She finally was in a coma for several days, suffering from congestive heart failure and struggling for life. She didn't know any of us.

Once after I left her hospital bedside, I was thinking to myself that she would be much better off if God would just go ahead and take her. Yet several days later, when my brother Leamon called and said that Mom had just died, I broke down and cried for several minutes. I was relieved in a way that she had died, yet at the same time my heart was broken. The news of her death brought back so many thoughts and memories of appreciation, of the love she had given to us so unselfishly, and now she was gone. Things would never be the same again. I had suffered an irreplaceable loss.

Indeed, at the time of this writing, I'm still working through my grief over the loss of my mother, who died on December 18, 1984. She was seriously ill two months before she passed on, and hers was a sort of slow death. Her family gathered around her very closely during those days, especially Dad, who was with her day and night at the hospital and at home. I don't think I ever saw Dad cry before that time. It was on a particular day when I was walking down the hallway with him from Mom's room. He broke down talking about Mom and how seriously ill she was. I think he was beginning to realize that she wasn't going to go home again.

One incident that took place during the final sickness of my mother was similar to experiences I've heard many times from those who are grieving. It involved a decision that we had to make regarding her. She was in a small-town hospital. Her doctor thought she would be better off in a larger hospital in Nashville. Yet he was reluctant to move her because he wasn't sure she could make the trip without having another heart attack. So he left the decision to us.

As he, Dad, and I finished our conversation, I asked the doctor what he would do if it were his mom. He said he didn't know. Some forty-five minutes later, Dad called me back into the hospital conference room to confer with the doctor and himself. The doctor said he had been thinking about my question and that his answer was that if she were his mom, he would take her to Nashville. He still said he wasn't sure she could make it; yet he knew she didn't have a chance by staying where she was.

I remember saying to Dad that he shouldn't blame himself if the decision turned out wrong because it might be wrong whatever we decided. If she stayed in the small hospital and died, we would always wonder if we should have taken her to Nashville. If we started with her to Nashville and she died, we would blame ourselves for not leaving her where she was. So it was a situation where we could be wrong with either decision. We finally decided to take her to Nashville. She made the trip well and was able to return to the small-town hospital before dying a few weeks later.

Several days before Mom died, she was in a coma part of the time and partially out of the coma at other times. Though in a coma, she would sometimes talk, and she often quoted Scripture. The Twenty-third Psalm was one of her favorites: "The Lord is my shepherd, I shall not want." That passage will always be especially meaningful to me because of this. Another remarkable thing during this time was that she would raise her hands up when she was in a convulsion and say over and over again, "Preach it from the mountain tops; preach it from the mountain tops." Her dad was a preacher, and four of her sons are preachers. Those statements will always motivate us to tell others of God's love and His salvation through Jesus.

Following the funeral and for more than a year after, I had a number of dreams about Mom. I thought I had been ready to give her up, and I still think I was. I knew that she would be better off going on than staying. Yet, I continued to hurt a great deal.

In August 1985, one of my brothers mentioned to me that Dad had been "dating" someone. At the time I didn't say anything, but I was hurt and shocked. I wasn't ready for it at all. I knew it wasn't wrong, but I was still involved in grief work involving Mom. I didn't think too much about it until later. Then one night in September, I received a call from another brother who told me that Dad was planning to get married the next day. This was about nine months after Mom's death. At the time, I was thinking about Mom's birthday, which was on the next day. It was very difficult for me to think about Dad's marrying someone else and about her being in the house that Mom had been in most of my life. I've heard so many other people talk about this and wondered why it was so hard to accept. It had nothing to do with not liking the other woman or having anything against her at all. I just wasn't ready for it, no matter who the woman was. I guess you never would be, but Mom's memory was still very active in my life, and it was difficult for me to accept. In fact, Dad had been married 11 days before I was able to accept his remarriage enough to call him and talk about it.

Grieving Over Mother

So on and on this struggle goes. I'm telling you some details about this because I've heard so many people who are grieving talk about similar struggles that are reflected in their dreams and relationships. They will dream about a departed mate. He will appear and start coming toward them. They will get close to him with outstretched arms, and then all of a sudden he vanishes. This sort of thing is an example of

4

one's trying to work things out subconsciously. Perhaps the widow in this case wanted so much to see him again and to take care of some unfinished business—to tell him especially that she loved him—that she produced the situation in her dreams that would allow her to do this. Yet, even subconsciously she wasn't able to carry it out. She knew that it was impossible to do so.

Another reason for explaining all of this is that it reflects the deep nature of grief. We can say that something doesn't matter, but our dreams say something different. They're more true to how we feel than what we may say. It does take quite a while for most people to work through their grief, to detach in a healthy way from that person who has died and be ready to form new relationships.

Finally, I tell you all of this so you'll understand that my interest in and experience with grief aren't just academic. I've suffered the loss and the pain that many of you are suffering now. Knowing what it's like both personally and as a counselor, I think I can help.

Researchers have developed several theories to explain grief. One deals with what writers call "separation anxiety", and another with "energy". However, the theory that consistently makes the most sense to me is the "loss" theory. The idea is that any time we lose something important to us, we grieve. Our thoughts, feelings, and activities are changed as the consequence of the loss of a loved one or of something we consider valuable. Grief can come from the trauma of being transferred to another city, from the loss of a job, the loss of one's health, the loss of a mate by divorce, or from any other losses. However, probably the most common grief is that which comes from the loss of a loved one by death.

Another helpful perspective focuses on the sense of separation from a person or an object of desire. This separation causes a reaction similar to anxiety, even a severe attack of anxiety. One writer points out that abnormal grief is made up of five elements: "Somatic distress [physical problems], preoccupation with the image of the deceased, guilt, hostile reactions, and loss of patterns of conduct."[1] I've found that some of these reactions are also experienced by people who are going through the normal stages of grief. This separation view of grief implies the need for creating new relationships in a supportive community of empathic people. The loss idea, on the other hand, points more to the past and to the loss of someone or something that was very important to us.

A third understanding of grief looks at it in terms of the emotion that's involved in the work of mourning. During the time of mourning, an individual seeks to disengage himself from a relationship that has existed and reinvest in new persons and directions that point toward the future. The grief process must get underway so that healing can occur. Grief work not only begins, but it also ends.

Perhaps something can be said for all these views of grief. Grief is a reaction to the loss of someone or something very important to us; it is a separation from something or someone to whom we were emotionally attached; and grief's purpose is to detach and to reinvest in new relationships. One must be able to separate from the past and move toward reinvestment in the future.

Broadly speaking, there are three types of grief: normal grief; morbid grief, which distorts normal grief; and anticipatory grief, which is normal grief that occurs before the loss is actually experienced. Most of the people who have participated in my grief therapy groups are experiencing normal grief. Though normal, it occasionally seems abnormal to those experiencing it. At times they think they're "going crazy."

A person's grief may be affected by at least four factors: personality structure, social factors, the value structure of the individual, and the relationship of the individual to the deceased. A dependent person will respond differently from an independent person. An emotional person will express pain differently from an intellectually oriented, stoic person. One with an obsessive personality and a history of depression is more likely than others to develop an agitated depression. A person with a strong, well-functioning social network is more likely than others to adjust well to a loss. He has lost a key person in his social system, yet others are there to take up the slack. This social network will influence the intensity and duration of the grief experience. The same is true of religious hope. Hope heals. The healthy personality usually bounces back.

How This Book Will Help You

With that brief introduction to grief and my experience with it, let me explain how this book is designed to help you grow through your own grief.

In the next chapter, we'll consider the importance of talking things out as you go through the grieving process. We'll discuss how and why this helps, and who can be most helpful to you.

There are some fairly predictable stages to the grieving process as most of us go through it, and Chapters 3-5 will explore these in detail. You'll be strengthened by better understanding what's happening to you, and by realizing your experiences and feelings aren't unusual.

Chapters 6-7 are meant primarily for those of you who want to counsel more wisely with others who are grieving However, you who are still grieving yourselves will also find much help there.

Because I've seen how helpful grief recovery groups can be, Chapter 8 is an explanation of how they work and how they can be set up and run. Perhaps after reading this book you'll want to help establish such groups in your own area.

Finally, in the last chapter we'll tie everything together and see how the principles here can begin helping you *immediately* in your passage through grief.

Join me now as we look at one of the best things you can do to deal with grief.

2

TALK IT OUT

If you've recently suffered the loss of a loved one, do you find that others are reluctant to talk about it? Many widows and widowers have told me, "My children don't want me to talk. They tell me it's time to put that in the past, but I *want* to talk about it. It's on my mind all the time anyway. Why *not* talk about it? They act as if he [or she] never existed, and *that* hurts. My friends act like that, too."

People who've said such things recognize almost instinctively the emotional value of talking about a departed loved one and their feelings for that person and for life in general at that point. Others, however, prefer to keep their thoughts and feelings bottled up inside. They're afraid of what people may think; they feel others don't care; they fear losing control; or if they're men, they may think it's not manly to cry or otherwise express deep emotion openly.

But expressing your thoughts and feelings openly, talking them out and crying if you feel like it, is one of the best things you can do to deal with your grief. Keeping it all bottled up inside just isn't healthy and makes the grieving process last longer than it otherwise would.

Why and How Talking Helps

Talking to someone else during your grieving helps first just because it gives you an outlet for your strong feelings. God made us as social creatures, needing contact and communication with others. And like the widows and widowers quoted at the beginning of this chapter, if you're grieving, those feelings are very much on your mind as you talk with another person. It's only natural to want to talk about something that's so important to you, and it's frustrating when you don't have an opportunity to do so.

Talking about it is also helpful because it's extremely important for you to know that there's at least one person who understands what you're going through and who accepts you and your feelings. You don't want to feel isolated while you're grieving. It's important that you have that connection to others in which you have the freedom to say what you're really thinking and feeling, knowing the subject won't get changed out of discomfort or you won't be rejected because you're not pleasant to be around.

Not only will talking help you find reassurance that you're still loved, understood, and accepted, but the thoughtful listening of the other person also acknowledges that it's okay for you to still be grieving. It's all right for you to still be working through the feelings. Different people work through grief at different rates, and you don't have to put it behind you overnight. Your life can be put back together gradually, piece by piece. A willing listener gives this freedom to you.

It's also a great help to feel that someone is sharing your burden of grief. You want to know that you're not the only one still thinking about and mourning for your loved one who died. Besides that, it's just easier to get through any difficult time or experience if you know someone else is going through it with you, shoulder to shoulder. As the Bible says in Proverbs 27:17, "Iron sharpeneth iron; so a man sharpeneth the countenance of his friend."

Next, talking about your feelings will help you sort through them, get a little more perspective on them, and perhaps gain some insight into them. Have you ever noticed how you can get an idea about something, and then as you begin to talk to a friend about it, different aspects of it or a different perspective on it will emerge? The person listening to you doesn't need to say much if anything, either. Your own words trigger your thought processes.

There's just something about explaining an idea, a problem, or a feeling out loud to another person that gives you a new angle on it and that makes it possible for you to see it in a fresh light. This seems to happen no matter how much thought you may have given to the matter before you began to discuss it.

That phenomenon of conversation, as we might call it, can be especially valuable to you as you're grieving, because your strong emotions can greatly color your thoughts and your perspective. Talking it all through, however, can help clarify your feelings and your situation.

An important part of dealing with grief is to remember good times with the deceased, his strong points as well as his weak. Your focus can't stay on the pain of your loss all the time. Part of the coping is to recall and to be thankful for the enjoyable times you shared, the things you appreciated about the other person, both big and small. And talking helps to bring these out. Often as you're describing one memory, another that's somehow connected to it will come to mind, and soon a whole chain of happy remembrances can brighten your day.

Finally, part of the grieving process is to face the future and think about the changes that your loss is going to bring to your life. This can be difficult, and it may take a little while before you're ready to deal with it. But eventually you must get to this point, and talking it out will greatly help you to do it.

Talking through the changes and the future with a good listener will assist you in gaining a measure of objectivity about them. If you're grieving over someone who was especially close to you, it may seem at first that you can't go on, that the future no longer holds any purpose. But in time as you talk with a caring, accepting person, you'll realize that life goes on and that God still has much that's good in store for your life.

To Whom Do You Talk?

I trust you can see now why it will be beneficial to you to talk to someone about your thoughts and feelings during your time of grief. But then the question arises, to whom do you talk? Although your tendency will be to reach out to the first person who indicates a willingness to listen, you should choose a confidant with some care. After all, during conversations in a time of grief, you'll be expressing deep feelings and perhaps also intimate confidences.

The first quality you need in a conversationalist, of course, is someone who'll listen and accept you regardless of what you say. In other words, you need to find someone who will be a true friend, who will let you speak your mind without interrupting and without judging.

Second, you need someone who can and will keep a confidence. You need the assurance that the person with whom you share your deep feelings isn't going to be spreading them to anyone else. Simply put, you want a person you can trust.

Third, it's good if the person is not only sympathetic, but also empathetic, one who can feel with you as you relive the experience. Perhaps the most helpful listener you can find is someone who has already gone through the grief you're now experiencing. Such a person not only feels bad *for* you, but also feels bad *with* you because he has been through the same thing and knows what the feelings and thoughts are like first hand. This friend can offer insights into your situation that might take you much longer to find on your own. Later, you can be this same type of friend for someone else.

Finally, it should go without saying that the person in whom you confide should share your religious convictions. The grieving process is not a time to get into a debate or to worry that your beliefs are being undermined. And part of the help that a listener should be able to give is the assurance that God's love and comfort are with you still.

If you're fortunate, you already have a friend or relative who possesses these qualities and who will be glad to talk with you. But if you don't, there are other sources of help. For example, a minister, a psychologist, or some other trained counselor might be your answer.

Don't automatically assume, however, that every professional counselor will meet your need. Look for the above qualities in evaluating these people as well. There is no shortage of professional help to choose from, so you should be able to find one with whom you feel comfortable.

Don't be ashamed of seeking professional help, either. We all have times in our lives when our load may become too much to bear alone, and a period of grief is certainly likely to be one of those occasions. Professional counselors are there to help at precisely those times.

Finally, let me recommend another source of help that I hope is available where you live. I'm referring to grief recovery groups such as the ones I've conducted over the past few years. As I said in the Preface, these have proved to be enormously helpful to the men and women who have taken part in them. The warmth, sharing, insight, and reassurance that a group of people going through the same experience can offer each other is amazing.

If there are such groups meeting where you live, please give one a try. Your minister or a counselor should be able to tell you if they are available. I'll have more to say about such groups in Chapter 8.

Wherever and with whomever you find the opportunity to talk and be heard, please avail yourself of this outlet for your thoughts and feelings. Don't keep everything bottled up inside. Your time of grief can be much easier to bear and to get through if you'll reach out and talk. It will also be made much easier if you understand the grief process you're going through, which the next chapter begins to discuss.

3

STAGES OF GRIEF, PART I

Ever since the publication of *On Death and Dying* by Elizabeth Kübler-Ross in 1969, it has been common to attempt to divide grief into stages. Kübler-Ross's stages of denial and isolation, anger, bargaining, depression, and acceptance apply primarily to one who is facing his own death, though there are similarities between these stages and the stages of the grief-recovery process. Various authors have attempted to divide the process into four, five, or ten stages, but all are trying to describe a process in which people "emotionally detach . . . from that which is now lost, thus enabling them to reinvest themselves in new attachments."[1]

I am reluctant to talk about stages of grief because I have never seen a list of stages, including my own list, that adequately describes the grief process of every individual. This is true because each person is different and the circumstances of each death are different. It is also true because the grief process doesn't always seem to happen in a linear fashion. Often, rather, it seems to go in circles.

Some try to allow for this by speaking of regressions. At times, perhaps even years after the loved one's death, the grief process is severe again, very much as it was right at first. Typically, however, if grief work is successfully done, such times will be fairly infrequent, and the grief of each regression will be less severe.

15

Still, even with these qualifications, it's very helpful to look at grief in a series of stages through which most people go. In my counseling, I've found that there are usually ten of these stages and that these ten stages are usually divided into three distinct parts. Part I encompasses *shock, lamentation,* and *withdrawal.* Part II encompasses *frustration, panic,* and *depression.* Part III encompasses *detachment, adaptation, reinvestment,* and *growth.* This chapter and the two following are devoted to describing these so you can better understand what you or someone for whom you care is experiencing. And please bear in mind that while much of the discussion that follows is written in third person for ease of expression, I'm trying to help *you* get a better grip on *your* grief.

Shock

It is hard to distinguish between shock and denial as the first stage of grief. Sometimes denial seems to precede shock, and at other times the order seems to be reversed. Denial seems to be not so much a stage as a protective response of the person who is in the grieving process. This response may come at any particular time during grief; it just doesn't ever seem to leave completely. "I cannot believe that my mother is dead." "I can see my wife when I come home from work at night." "My husband talks to me even though I know he is gone." These are common reactions by people at various times during their grieving process. Denial continues for months and sometimes even for years.

The process of grief is triggered by learning of the death of someone you love. Shock and denial are normal reactions that serve as a buffer zone between no grief and grief. As one realizes the loss, there are "waves of emotion and responses" that may overwhelm the person to the point of immobility.

There may be changes within the body such as heart palpitations, dizziness, tightness in the throat and muscles, loss of appetite, a sensation of numbness and tingling, and fainting. The person feels stunned, dazed, and overwhelmed. What is happening seems unreal. The person is confused, tense, and apprehensive.

In this stage, one feels anesthetized. It is as though the brain were saying to the body that things are too much. "I can't take it any more." It almost seems that the person is being shielded from an understanding of the magnitude of the loss. At this point, there is very little rational thinking that takes place. One is not ready to receive heavy bits of advice.

Shock is a stage of emotion. The person vacillates between bewilderment and anger, helplessness and hostility, confusion and rage. He may turn incommunicative and impulsive, and he may continue to deny that this is really happening to him. He may even try to cut off his feelings during the crisis and become quite calloused; yet he is overwhelmed. His system just cannot accept the truthfulness of the event into consciousness.

A person in this stage may act very much like a child, crying and screaming without disguise or inhibition. Or he may take another approach and clam up. Men especially have difficulty with tears. Crying can be thought of as a gift from God, however—a gift that helps us return to normal.

This dream-like state infused with suffering may last from a few moments to several days. A person during this time may experience bizarre behavior and emotions. One widow, for example, said that she felt so full that she just wanted to explode. Her reaction was to go into the bathroom and scream at the top of her lungs. After she did this, she thought that anyone who screamed like that must be going crazy. Yet this is normal behavior for one who is grieving.

Another widow described her emotions as being mechanical. She came in from grocery shopping one day, put toilet tissue in the refrigerator, and did not notice it until later. At a later date, when she discovered what she had done she felt as if she were "losing my marbles." Yet this, too, is common behavior for those who are in a state of shock. In my book *Mental Health and the Bible*, I summarized features of the shock stage as follows:

> One may feel . . . sorry for himself, frustrated, disinterested, alone. One may withdraw from people, become aggressive, cry profusely, clam up, bottle up grief, do strange things, deny the death, distort the truth by claiming perfection for the one who has died. Restlessness, loss of sleep, and failure to eat properly . . . are common.[2]

There may be all kinds of additional physical symptoms such as perspiration, tightness in the chest, pain in the heart, upset stomach, headaches, and even sickness itself. In fact, many who are grieving experience more sickness than at other times—often twice as much during the first year of grieving. This is measured by hospital visitations, medications taken, and trips to physicians.

Even though typical behavior in the shock stage seems strange, it serves a purpose. Perhaps the Semitic society knew something when they spent special times alone before the funeral. At that point, the person really does not feel like visiting with anyone. Guests could come at a later date when the person feels more like talking. Often in our American society, we leave people alone when they need to be visited and visit them when they need to be alone.

Lamentation

I have labeled the second stage of grief "lamentation" because this is often a time of anger, hostility, lament, and protestation. As was mentioned earlier, the Semitic culture encouraged lamentation. The Old Testament has several examples of it. Why did Abner, Saul's general, have to die when he did? It didn't seem fair to David who lamented for Abner and said:

> "Should Abner have died as a fool dieth? Thy hands were not bound, nor thy feet put into fetters: as a man falleth before wicked men, so fellest thou." And all the people wept again over him. And when all the people came to cause David to eat meat while it was yet day, David swore, saying, So do God to me, and more also, if I taste bread, or aught else, "till the sun be down" (2 Samuel 3:33-35).

The nature of a lament is to express disappointment, anger, and strong feelings. Almost everyone who has studied grief has indicated that something like this takes place. I believe it occurs rather early in the grieving process and may continue for a number of months, overlapping many other stages of grief. Sometimes the expression of anger will be accompanied by profuse crying. God gave us tear glands, and we're supposed to use them. If we cannot use them when we lose someone we love, what are they for?

Anger is sometimes very irrational. It may be directed at the deceased for leaving the person burdened down with many responsibilities and frustrations. The person grieving may feel hurt and betrayed by the one who has died, though seldom do I see this. Later, such a person may feel guilty because of such feelings.

Sometimes a person is angry with himself because of things he did or did not do during the lifetime of the person who has died. "I wasn't nice to him." "I didn't say good-bye to him on the night he died." "I didn't get him to the hospital on time." "I didn't take him to the right doctor." Often, there is a thin line between guilt feelings and anger at oneself. "I talked to him in a nasty way." "I wish I hadn't treated him the way I did." Anger, however, can be a positive sign if it helps move one beyond being stuck in a state of sadness and depression.

The person grieving may be angry not only at the deceased but also at the doctor and nurses. "They didn't do everything they could have done to make him well." "They didn't even tell me what was going on." "They should have been nicer to him." "They should have told me to take him somewhere else." "I told them he was too weak for an operation." All these are common thoughts in the minds of those who are grieving. Sometimes anger is also directed at the ambulance driver. He didn't get them to the hospital fast enough. "If he had gone a little faster, my husband would not have died."

Hostility, which is common at this stage, is a tendency to respond with irritability and a wish not to be bothered by others. Sometimes I have seen the grieving person direct hostility and anger toward God for allowing his loved one to die. "How could He allow this to happen?" "If He really cared, He could have and would have intervened."

At times, the minister is blamed. He didn't visit the hospital enough, or he said the wrong thing at the funeral.

Sometimes others who try to comfort the grieving person are blamed. Anger is directed at them for saying the wrong things. "You can get another child." "You are still young. You can get married again." "You ought to be thankful for having such a wonderful husband for so many years. Mine died when I was only forty." "You are a man.

It's easier for a man." These statements, though well-intended, seldom help. The person grieving thinks that such a person doesn't really understand how much he is hurting.

Each grieving person is different. A statement that will make one person mad will encourage another. It is very hard to know what to say. At any rate, I think of protestation and anger as natural. I will admit, however, that I have not seen this manifested as often as would be indicated by other writers.

Anger toward the deceased themselves, especially, is seldom expressed by those who are grieving. It is a real exception in my opinion. In such cases, usually a person "smoked himself to death" or "drank himself to death." The one who is left behind feels cheated by the one who died. Somehow, it was his fault that he died. However, if a person dies of natural causes, the griever seldom thinks of his dying as being his fault and is not mad at him because of his death.

Anger toward God and toward the medical profession are fairly common, however, I have heard a number of grievers express such anger and protest that all of this is not fair. "Why should he die at this point?" "I needed him." "We had a house on the lake. He had just retired. It just doesn't seem to be fair." These protests are quite similar to David's back there in 2 Samuel.

The physical reactions mentioned earlier will continue throughout this stage. As the days pass, however, these symptoms will gradually disappear until the bereaved person recovers.

In some cases, though, grief can cause more than temporary reactions. It can become a major source of illness and distress of the body, mind, and spirit. These illnesses aren't mere symptoms of the diseases that killed the loved one but are illnesses and distresses in themselves. Grief even seems to be able to kill by means of breaking hearts.

During this time of lamentation, the grieving person may experience various hallucinations as well as a strong preoccupation with the image of the deceased. He just cannot get the deceased out of his mind. One writer says that fifty percent or more of those who mourn have hallucinations. I remember a widow who continued to talk about seeing her husband floating face down in the lake where she had found him after he died. It was very difficult for her to get this scene out of her mind.

Hallucinations may involve sight, smell, touch, or sound of the deceased as experienced by the bereaved. He may think the deceased is present. In fact, this has been often experienced by those in our groups. One widow said that her husband had reappeared in her bedroom several nights before but that her friends thought she was crazy.

I encouraged her to tell us what she was talking about, and she did. She said that her husband used to smoke, which scared her a great deal because she was afraid he would catch the bed on fire. On the night of the hallucination, she had been dreaming about him, and when she awakened, the smell of smoke was in the room. She just knew that he was present. The smell was very real. I believe that her dream had touched the stored memory of the smell of smoke. She *did* smell the smoke as though he were there. This explanation seemed to help her understand what was going on and to adjust to the situation.

Hallucinations, though a normal and healthy part of the grieving process, can be very disturbing to the bereaved. One researcher found that the most common type of hallucinations are those in which there is a sense of the presence of the deceased; that widows under forty are less prone to hallucinations; that widows who have been widows less than ten years are more prone to hallucinations; that people who were happily married are more prone to hallucinations than were those who were unhappily married; and that there was a significant decrease in hallucinations if the marriage had been childless.[3]

However irritating all the feelings and experiences of the lamentation stage may be, one should not be discouraged from protesting. It seems to be helpful; it seems to be natural. Even if one is protesting against God, we have illustrations of this in the Bible. The positive thing about those illustrations is that they often led to a greater faith in God. Job protested but then turned to a greater trust in God. He never did completely understand the reason for his losses, but he continued to trust in God. I suppose that's what real faith is all about.

If people don't get the feelings of this stage out of their system, they nevertheless remain a reality. And a person is more likely to work through those feelings of anger, hostility, and protest if he expresses what he's feeling rather than bottling it up. In fact, refusing to let these emotions out complicates the symptoms I have been discussing. I remember a widow, referred to me by her medical doctor, with a rash all over her body. The doctor thought it was caused by her bottling up her grief. After a few weeks of opening up and discussing her feelings about her deceased husband, the rash went away, and she felt much better.

Thus, it is extremely beneficial to have a healthy discussion of one's anger, hostilities, feelings of guilt, and other memories that may be damaging. It is amazing how we can convince ourselves of all kinds of things concerning a loved one. If you are grieving, I encourage you again to talk it out. If you are trying to help someone else, I encourage you to listen to him. Such discussion is a vital way of working through grief to greater understanding, to readjustment, to reinvestment in life, and to becoming a stronger person.

Withdrawal

Withdrawal is another stage that's almost universal. Some withdraw longer and more completely than do others, yet everyone seems to use withdrawal as a response to the loss of a loved one.

Grief sometimes changes a person's lifestyle and personality. Pain becomes overwhelming. There is a feeling of dejection, a loss of interest, an inhibition of activities, panic, hostility toward one's self, and other signs of low self-esteem.

There may be some shame and change of self-image when a loved one dies. This is especially true when prospective parents have a stillborn child. The mother may lose her view of herself as a mother, and the father may lose his view of himself as a man who is able to father a child. Even their sex life may be affected, since sex is now connected with death and shame.

Our society conditions us to be quiet in the face of death. Doctors and nurses often do not talk about it. Death is made to seem like something for which we should be ashamed. Self-esteem is lost. We are hurt. And "maybe I'm to blame."

Immediately after the funeral, a grieving person often withdraws to himself. He may not go to work. He may not go to church. He usually avoids social activities. "No, no, no. I don't want to go. I'm not interested! I just don't have any purpose in life any more. I don't feel like getting up in the morning. I don't feel like cooking. There's no one to cook for. What's the use?"

The withdrawal stage is a time for being alone, a time for reflection over one's own life and the life of the deceased, a time for evaluation of just where one is in life. All the time the grieving person is hurting, yet this is a necessary stage toward recovery. One cannot go forward and make new attachments until he knows where he is in relationship to old attachments. "Just where does this leave me? Who am I *now*? Am I a widow, a wife, a mother, a single, married—just who am I? And can I accept myself as I am *now*?"

Sometimes one's social status is greatly changed when a mate dies. Take, for example, a widow of a prominent physician. She had never worked outside the home. "He brought all of the glory, money, and prestige to our home, and now he's gone," she said. "I'm just a nobody. My usual crowd does not invite me to the social gatherings anymore. They just liked me because I was a part of my husband, and now he's gone." These thoughts may persist for days. They are very real and hard to face. One faces them by pulling away for a time and taking stock.

As the shock from a death wears off, one tends to avoid facing reality at all costs. A person laments and withdraws. He refuses visits and avoids references to the deceased. Self-control is often maintained and reinforced by family, friends, ministers, and funeral directors. He feels distant from people and from self. Yet he believes he is in control, and he thinks that's very important to him and to others. After all, one is out of control when one cries, expresses anger, paces the floor, or idealizes the deceased. He should get it together, and he does; he does not fret. He has faith, and he does not cry. He will control himself. He will repress his grief. He is in control. Yet the grief cannot be controlled. It brings about additional illnesses, personality changes, and social maladjustment. To control his anger, he represses it, and then it controls him.

During this time of withdrawal, the grieving person faces many strange experiences. He feels humiliated and deprived because of the loss. Yet, when sorrow is *really felt*, grief work begins. He is often apathetic and withdrawn. He ignores demands, decisions, and conversations. He feels helpless and avoids responsibilities. He may appear irrational at times. Yet in all of this, the necessary work of grief is usually continuing, even if progress is hard for others to see.

During all this time, certain feelings and behaviors may continue from earlier stages. The griever may still feel guilty because of something he did or failed to do. He then tries to compensate by glorifying the deceased, remembering only his good points. He is angry. He is preoccupied with the image of the deceased, at times believing that he is still present. Hallucinations continue to be normal experiences at this stage as well.

Other manifestations of grief during this time may include a loss of warmth toward other people, aggression toward specific persons, and simplification of complex facts and ethical behavior. "God is punishing him because of his sin." "He died because I once wished he were dead." "Older people have to die before the young."

During withdrawal, the person grieving may try in a sense to "resurrect" the deceased. He does this in various ways: by an effort to make permanent what the deceased had to offer (carrying out his work), or by adopting certain characteristics and behaviors of the deceased. If none of this brings relief, one may "go to pieces" in order to stay together. If none of this works, a person seems to withdraw further and the process continues. He seems to say, "If I can't bring you back, I'll die myself." And then he almost does.

Yet, withdrawal has a purpose. A person must reflect in order to know where he is, and he must in order know where he is before he can go forward to a meaningful life. He does not leave the stage of withdrawal abruptly. Rather, he leaves for a time and then returns. There may, in fact, be times of withdrawal for years to come; yet these times normally become less frequent after a few weeks, and the adverse experiences also become less severe. Thus there is hope when you feel like dying. When you hit the bottom, there is no way to go but up.

4

STAGES OF GRIEF, PART II

We've looked so far at the first three stages of grief: shock, lamentation, and withdrawal. As we consider in this chapter the next three stages, remember that everyone experiences grief a little differently. Just what you feel and do, how long you stay in a certain stage, or whether you even experience a particular stage—all depend on you as an individual. So don't be surprised or concerned if you don't match the model exactly.

Frustration

The fourth common grief stage is frustration. There are often some frustrations before the funeral. Where will he be buried? Who should be called? Who will conduct the funeral? What about the casket? These and many other questions must be answered early during one's grief experience.

Yet during these first few days, there are usually other people present to make or help make such decisions. Some things just have to be done, and we do them. Others help, and we make the decisions that must be made even though we may just be going through the motions.

One widow said to me that she didn't remember any of the songs that were sung at her husband's funeral. Others remember and are continually strengthened by them and by the message of the minister. I went with one widow to help her pick out a casket, and she acted as though she were in a daze. She couldn't decide anything. But somehow she got through it all. Some do it with help from sedatives, but at least they survive.

Although in my studies, I have never seen the word frustration used to represent a stage, I am using it because it represents something that is very real to hundreds of grieving people with whom I have worked. At some point after the funeral, grieving persons are faced with many difficult decisions and unfamiliar chores. The list is endless: collecting the insurance, paying funeral bills, probating the will, paying taxes, taking care of banking accounts, getting into bank vaults, getting everything put into your name, selling property, repairing cars and houses, mowing the grass, parenting, washing clothes, cleaning up the house, cooking, coping with loneliness, getting a job, perhaps dating, and the list goes on and on.

Specific new tasks differ somewhat for widows and widowers, but the list is still significant. The widow does not know how to repair the roof or mow the grass, and the widower may not be able at first to use the dishwasher or to cook. Details vary from person to person, but you get the idea. Everyone is faced with something that he or she did not handle previously, and it is frustrating. The more dependent on the deceased a person was, the more frustrated he or she becomes. It is tough!

One widower said that he did not know what powder to put into the washing machine and wondered how one could lose so many socks while washing clothes. This was one question the widows could not help him with. The best they could do was to just say that the washing machine eats them. A widow became overwhelmed when so many details faced her all at once. She could not get into her husband's bank vault because it was in his name. The will had to be probated first. Yet she needed the money to pay bills. Income taxes were due, and she had never "filled out all those papers before." So many things were happening. One day she got an obscene phone call, and she "just went to pieces." That was the straw that broke the camel's back for her.

Frustrations come at different times during the grief period. I do not know exactly where to put this stage because it continues for months, and to some extent throughout the grieving process. I'm not sure that frustration should even be called a stage. Yet it fits so many things I have heard grievers describe that I am calling it a stage. And I put it at this point in the process because the frustrations snowball not too long after the funeral. So I just say that there is a frustration stage and that it is normal.

Financial difficulties are mentioned often by widows. "We thought we were okay, but we didn't plan on his dying. He made most of the money, and we have very little saved and very little insurance. I've got to look for a job, and I have no job skills, haven't worked since we married. I'm not even sure how much we have. He had some bank accounts and investments, but I'm not sure where they all are or how much is in them." These are statements I have heard often from widows. Where do they go from here? Because these financial frustrations are so common, I offer the following suggestions.

First, find out where you stand. Contact banks, places of your husband's employment, the Veterans Administration, the Social Security Administration, insurance agents, close friends of your husband, and others. Ask questions, and make a list of your assets: savings, checking accounts, insurance, retirement, bonds, dividends, property, stocks, and so on. What are your assets, liabilities, and net worth? The will must be probated before you know exactly where you are financially.

Second, what is your regular income? Include any salary you may have from work, Social Security benefits, pension payments, dividends, interest, and any other regular funds you receive. Figure out how much you will be getting each month.

Third, how much do you owe? What about the hospital, the doctors, and funeral expenses? What about other fixed expenses such as rent or mortgage, insurance, installment payments, taxes, church contributions, medication, and other items? You might also want to put some money each month into a retirement fund and some into an emergency fund for yourself. Many families like to have at least three months worth of wages in an emergency fund for unseen expenses such as accidents, unemployment, broken appliances, wrecked cars, sickness, and other unforeseen expenses. This is a good idea if you can at all do it.

Fourth, what are your flexible expenses? This category includes food, clothing, gasoline, medical care, entertainment, education, household expenses, and so on. These are flexible in that they usually can be either increased or decreased as necessary.

Fifth, what are your goals, your needs, your wants? Paying your bills should come first. Then come other items such as trips, extras around the house, and other optional items. Your goals will help you plan your budget. You want to be in charge, and this is the way to do it.

Sixth, determine how much you spend. Keep up with everything you spend for one month. Group your expenses under general categories such as food, transportation, clothing and laundry, housing, utilities, insurance, medical expenses, education, recreation, savings, and other items. Do not forget quarterly, semi-annual, and annual expenses.

Seventh, compare income with actual expenses. If you are spending more than you take in, some changes must be made. See where you can cut back; perhaps a purchase of clothing or a vacation can be postponed. If money is left over, put it into a savings fund to use at a later time toward some important goal.

Eighth, determine how you want to spend your money during the next year. Check your obligations, your needs, your wants, and your income. Money must be set aside for fixed debts and obligations as well as flexible needs and wants. Leave some money for that emergency fund.

Ninth, get out of debt as much as possible. List all your debts. How much do you owe each person or company? What is your monthly payment and what are the interest rates? If you cannot pay each creditor what you owe, figure out how much you *can* pay. Then go with this plan for every person and company you owe. Show them all your figures. If they say they are going to sue you, remind them that others may also sue and that there is just not enough money to go around at this point. Be open and honest, and then pay when you can.

Tenth, make a budget for the next year. Include income and expenditures for the various categories we've already mentioned. Include on your budget work sheet an amount planned for each item, the amount actually spent, and a place to list the difference between the two.

Finally, stick with your new budget if at all possible. This is the hard part. Many people are used to overspending. The total American debt is nearly 50 percent greater than the national debt. The typical American spends some 30 percent of his after-tax income for housing, 22 percent for food, 14 percent for transportation, 10 percent for medical needs, 9 percent for clothing and personal care, 7 percent for recreation, and 8 percent for other items.

In addition to money, another prominent source of frustration is the lack of sexual activity, something not readily discussed in groups. In fact, most of our groups have been reluctant to admit that such a problem exists. Yet it does. How does one participate in sexual activity during many years of marriage and then stop suddenly?

My main advice is for each person to think this problem through ahead of time and not let people use you. Go to places where you will meet people who are likely to be interested in *you* rather than merely in *sex*. Find other things to do. Some say that such activities as physical exercise, sports, the arts, and just having good friends have partially filled the void left by a lack of sex. Some masturbate, some have affairs.

Remember, your conscience must be considered. Your value system is important. Since the Bible plainly says that sex outside of marriage is wrong, I don't have any easy solution to the sexual adjustment problem for widows and widowers. Remarriage is the answer for some. Yet one should not rush into remarriage. Such decisions take time. And working through grief takes time.

Another frustration mentioned often by widows and widowers is social in nature. "Our old friends drop us. This world is couple-oriented. I feel like a fifth wheel. I just don't fit in. Wives of husbands I know are jealous of me. They think I'm interested in their husbands, and that's the furthest thing from my mind. I just hate to be dropped. Even social situations are organized for couples. I don't like to go out by myself, and I don't have anybody to go with." These are statements I have heard repeatedly. What's the answer?

Just say to yourself, *There is some truth in these thoughts, but that's not the whole picture. I can call up a friend and go out to lunch. Perhaps they're dropping me because of the way I've been acting. I'll call some friends and tell them I'm ready to be included in social life again. I'll do what I can about the situation.* Such thoughts will help you to succeed, to overcome social obstacles.

I'm not sure I would call dating a frustration, but it is awkward at first for most widows and widowers. They have forgotten how to flirt, how to act, how to talk romance to anyone who is not their mate. Also, at first they feel as though they are being disloyal to their deceased mate. "It's like I was stepping out on my husband," one widow said. I certainly can understand this, because I felt something similar toward my dad when I learned of his plan to remarry.

Widows and widowers usually learn to meet these and other frustrations one at a time. They learn in doing so that they can do many things that they never before thought they could. And they grow in the process.

Panic

The fifth stage in normal grief is called panic. I chose this word because I have heard so many grieving people use it. One said, "I just panicked. I couldn't face it. I realized that I was alone, and it was not going to change. He wasn't coming back. I felt the weight of the whole world on my shoulders. And I could feel it throughout my body. Even my hands trembled."

Pain during this period is very real and deep. The person is past feeling numb and is into suffering. There is a great deal of fear. "How can I go on? I just can't do it without her." "How am I going to make a living?" "What if I lose my other loved ones? I just can't face that." "What about my own death? I'm scared! I'm in bad health." "What's going to happen to me? I can't even drive. How can I make it? I'm afraid to die. Oh, I'd like to die sometimes, but it's not my time yet. I'm in a mess. What can I do?"

There is a feeling of despair. The situation seems hopeless. There is no comfort. Those who try to help often feel helpless and experience a sense of despair themselves.

There are many psychological reactions as stress is translated into bodily problems. We tend to moderate public expression of grief as time goes by; it is then repressed and continues to fester, thus causing further physiological problems. Some of the typical symptoms of panic are difficult respiration, palpitations of the heart, chest pain, choking sensations, dizziness, feelings of unreality, tingling in the hands or feet, perspiration, trembling or shaking, and various fears. Such pain is intense.

One writer says the work of grief through the panic stage lasts up to five or six weeks,[1] but I think it's usually much longer than that. In fact, panic symptoms may come and go for several years, although they usually continue for about six months.

Panic is experienced by many who grieve. Exactly where it should be placed in the process is debatable, but it is definitely a part of the process for many. Though it may be experienced at any time after the loss of a loved one, it more often comes either toward the first or near the middle of the grieving process.

Just establishing a state of relative calmness is the main task of this stage. Crying, physical exercise, and talking may help. Yet if panic symptoms persist, one should seek professional help. Then the grieving process can continue along its normal course toward recovery.

Depression

During the process of grief, there is a going down and a coming up; there is disorganization and reorganization; there is disintegration and a return to wholeness. In my ten stages of grief, there are six stages downward and four upward. Thus, depression takes us to the bottom.

Almost all reports on grief mention depression or symptoms similar to those produced by depression. It is a "down" feeling, a feeling of sadness, a sense of great loss. A depressed person is often passive, tired, and inactive. Symptoms of those grieving over the loss of a loved one are often very similar to those who are clinically depressed.

During this stage of depression, one constantly remembers the deceased. He relives the past over and over again, almost as though it will come out differently by such thoughts. His memory is often distorted and impaired during this time, and he sometimes forgets bad experiences or unpleasant characteristics of the departed loved one. He puts the loved one on a pedestal with constant idealizations. While this may help the griever with the anger and guilt he feels about the deceased, it may also hold up the grieving process.

The griever finally realizes that there is no hope of return for his departed loved one, and this is sad. He feels dejected and sometimes hopeless. Reality has finally set in.

The griever dwells upon the loss almost exclusively, and depression increases. He may realize that he must go on living, but now he doesn't feel like doing so.

Pictures and other items of the loved one are constant reminders of the griever's loss, proving that part of him is gone. Efforts to cheer up someone in this stage or to encourage activities in order to get his mind on something else may do harm rather than good. Merely listening is a more appropriate response. Depressed persons usually do not talk freely, however; and if they do, they are usually negative in what they say: "I'm alone. My life is not worth living, and it's not going to get any better. Nobody needs me. They wouldn't even miss me if I died. I'm just in the way. I don't eat well. I don't know what's going to happen to me."

One is overcome by waves of sadness and loneliness. There are nights of agitated and restless sleep, loss of appetite, often a feeling of disorganization, and a loss of interest and ability to take care of the affairs of everyday life.

Because of such intense feelings of sadness, it is probably best, if possible, to postpone important decisions for at least a year after the loss of a close relative. Selling property is an example of such a decision. Marriage is another. There are exceptions, but it usually takes people at least a year to recover from a significant loss. Decisions made during the grieving process are often bad decisions. Later, one is more rational.

Whether or not one is clinically depressed during grief may be debatable. However, I do know that many of the symptoms of clinical depression are experienced by those who grieve. They are very sad. They are almost always passive. Grievers at this stage often become very inactive: they stay in bed, don't cook, don't clean the house, don't go to church. They just don't feel like doing anything. And it's a vicious cycle: the more depressed a person gets, the more inactive he gets; and the more inactive he gets, the more depressed he becomes. Some in our groups have talked of suicide, and this always gets my attention. One woman said she came to the group because the day before she "went down to the bridge and almost jumped off, and that scared me. I thought, I must need help, so I came." She further said that the one thought that kept her from doing it was the statement in 2 Corinthians 12:9: "My grace is sufficient for thee." She said that at the moment she did not feel it, but that she "trusted in the Lord to do what He said." So, she carried on. Now, several years later, this fine woman is still very much alive and doing well.

I am not sure that everyone who grieves gets depressed. Everyone who has lost someone whom he loves experiences some of the symptoms of depression such as sadness and feelings of discouragement. And many are very depressed. This may come soon after the death and may last for several days or months. If severe depression persists for weeks, one should seek professional help.

Healthy people usually work through grief quite well. Those who have previously suffered from depression may experience more difficulty. The loss may trigger more severe depression that will need professional attention. The typical depression caused by grief is a reactive type of depression with a good prognosis for recovery.

If you are at a low point now, hang on. You cannot go any lower when you get to the bottom. And time may help you a great deal. Depression tends to go in cycles. God has given you additional life; He wants you to use it. There will be plenty of time to die "when your time comes."

Think of it this way: If you had died before your loved one, how would you want your loved ones to react? You would want them to express sorrow at the loss, to respect and appreciate your memory, and then to go on with their lives. That's what I want you to do. As a widower in one of our groups said, "I suddenly realized that I have some more leaves in my life's book to write." And you do, too. It takes strength and courage to write them, but you can do it. And you will be glad you did.

Stages of grief are mere steps toward readjustment and indeed toward growth. Though one would never wish to experience grief, I have seen a number of people who have grown as a result of working through it. They become more adequate as persons, they learn that they can do many things that they could not do before, and they develop personally. They just sort of continue to unfold as people and become stronger as a result of their grief. This, however, could not happen by denial. It is the result of courageous working through the grief. I wish for you health and strength and encouragement as you work through your grief or as you help others work through theirs.

5

STAGES OF GRIEF, PART III

In our movement through the first six stages of the grieving process, we've now reached the bottom of the emotional journey with depression. At this point, the road turns upward. The last four stages offer the hope that life can be meaningful and joyful again, and that a grieving person can even grow through the experience and emerge as a stronger individual.

Detachment

The grieving person is at the bottom. He is sad and miserable. He has lost his loved one, and the loved one is not coming back! He cannot seem to go on with his life because he is still very closely and tenaciously attached to his deceased loved one. The attachment holds him to the deceased. And before he can proceed with his life, this attachment must be weakened.

Detachment as I am using it here is not detachment from people in general, as is done in withdrawal, but rather detachment from the emotional bond with the deceased. Such detachment does not mean that one loves the deceased less; that doesn't change. It means rather that the living one is not constantly tied in thought and action to the deceased.

He detaches in the sense that he can think of other things. He can go on with his life. This stage is a middle step between attachment to the deceased and reinvestment in the lives of others. And it is a very necessary step.

I have not heard grievers use this word much in describing their lives, but they use similar concepts. "My life was still tied completely to the past. I had to think of other things. I couldn't just keep on moping around the house. I had to get out and go on with my life. So, I called up a friend and told her I wanted her to come over for coffee. I have enjoyed talking to her, and we have gone out to lunch together several times lately."

A widower said, "I finally realized that I had to do something. I went shopping, I bought groceries. And lately, I've been grocery shopping also for a shut-in widow across the street. I've got to look to the future, not just to the past. I'll always love my wife, but I know that she would not want me to keep on like I've been going."

That widower was displaying what one writer calls courage, the most important ingredient for working through grief. It takes much courage to examine and accept one's feelings continually as the wounds heal.

One cannot rush grief work. Yet if it isn't faced, it may be delayed for an extended period of time. Pressing responsibilities put grieving off. Even during such times, however, one often experiences an inhibited form of grief. Numerous somatic complaints accompany such grief. Children and older adults may be more likely to experience such inhibited reactions of grief than are others. But one finds that he cannot hide his grief forever. So, he gently forces himself back into action.

At this stage, one begins to make more rational decisions than were at first possible. He has allowed himself enough time to hurt, to be sad, to experience despair and loneliness. He begins to realize that he is still alive. He is not in the cemetery; his loved one's body is. He begins to pull away. His loved one is dead, and he is not to blame. He begins to talk more freely about his memories, his anger, and his life. He is beginning to let go of the hurt and pain. The psychic energy attached to the deceased is gradually detached and is thus free and available to utilize in one's life in the present. As C. S. Lewis expressed it, it's as if God is saying, "good, you have mastered that exercise, I am very pleased with it. And now you are ready to move on to the next."[1]

Detachment is characterized by emotional burnout and emotional feelings. It's a time of emotional lethargy. Although disorientation at this point is a possibility, it normally does not happen. As detachment from the deceased proceeds, positive actions may occur as the individual increasingly realizes he must go on living.

Detachment does not overcome loneliness. The griever continues to experience an inner loneliness even when with others.

It is also true that the mourner will sometimes regress. There are days when guilt feelings return, anger returns, and even denial momentarily returns. I still sometimes expect to see my mother-in-law when I visit my father-in-law, although she has been dead for more than three years. Perhaps it is conditioning and habit over the years rather than denial. Regardless, it is a very real experience.

An expression of one's emotions should be continually encouraged because such expression is a release of pressure. One fact I have learned for sure in my grief work is that it helps to face the grief squarely; it won't just go away by itself.

As one griever put it, the periods of intense mourning then tend to become shorter and less intense.

Relapses most often come on birthdays, holidays, anniversaries, or on other special days. My grief over my mother was recently revived by a letter I received from my sister, Linda. The letter caused me to rethink Mom's sickness and death; and that night, I dreamed that I was in the back seat of a huge car, and Dad was driving it. We proceeded very rapidly from Dad's front yard down the bank across the road through a fence, knocking it down. I just closed my eyes and said, "I've got to hang on." The car finally ran into a group of trees and stopped as I awakened rather terrified.

The next night, I had another very upsetting dream. The letter did not cause the grief. It merely triggered some more grief work, which took place in my dreams.

Although it's hard for me to determine why the particular settings were used by my subconscious mind for the grief work, it's easy for me to analyze the present content of the dreams. It is hard to go back. Mom is gone. I cannot go back to the way it used to be. Dad is in the driver's seat now. I love him and want to go with him. It may be hard, but I am in the back seat, closing my eyes and hanging on.

I suppose that analysis is fairly accurate. I am adjusting, yet I am still so attached to Mom that it hurts to see Dad remarried. I know, however, that this is his way of adjusting and going on with his life. In a large family so many different people are involved in the death of a beloved parent. Everyone may be at different points in the grieving process, and this causes some difficulty.

Relapses such as I have described will occur. And as one writer points out, "Only by recognizing that there will be relapses—times when all the raw distress of the acute phase returns in full force—can the impact of such times be softened and the occurrence be drained of its frightening nature."[1]

The time necessary for recovery varies from person to person so much so that I hesitate to speak of time as it relates to what I am calling stages. Yet time is a factor. Most people take some six months or more to get to this stage of detachment from the deceased. They still love the deceased; they are just not totally absorbed with him all the time. They thus are ready to adjust to life in the present.

Adaptation

I say I have adapted to my mom's death and to my dad's remarriage. Yet just last night while writing this, I had a dream that indicates a deep longing for her return. The dream opened up at the Flatt Cemetery near my mom's grave. There was a large crowd present, including several close relatives. As we began to leave the cemetery, I was thinking that Mom could not go with us; she would have to stay there. But in dreams all kinds of things are possible. Mom protested, saying that she wanted to go with us, so she did.

Later in the dream, I was plowing with a double shovel plow behind a mule. It was in a tobacco patch on our old home place. As I plowed, the dirt rolling toward the small tobacco plants evoked fear that I would cover up the smaller plants, but I had to get close enough to put some dirt near all the plants. It was a very real experience, just like the old days.

Then I noticed that Mom was helping Dad and the other boys to uncover the small plants that I had covered with dirt, to cut weeds, and to hoe more dirt around the big plants. I was afraid her heart wouldn't take such a strain, but she was deliberately bending all the way over to show us that she could do it. She said, "I know what you're thinking, but I can do it just as good as ever."

I know intellectually that she is not coming back but that I can go to her. Yet subconsciously, I brought her back. I still have Mom, and Dad doesn't need anyone else; he still has Mom, too, and she's as good as ever, at least in my dreams. This experience might be called yearning, and it usually occurs during the first few months after the death of a loved one. But in my case, it occurred months later.

I am detached from Mom to some extent. I go for hours without thinking of her. So I am able to adapt to life in a rather normal way. I am not completely back to normal, but people in my presence would probably think I am.

Adaptation to life follows detachment from the deceased—not complete detachment, which never happens, but detachment from a constant emotional pre-occupation with the deceased. One is thus able to adjust to his current situation.

Some writers refer to this stage as acceptance, and acceptance is a part of what happens here. But acceptance, in a sense, happens much earlier. You accept the death at the funeral, but you do not adapt to it. You just cannot keep on denying it.

Some sort of adjustment occurs even from the start. We go back home after the funeral and continue to exist. Readjustment occurs several months later, perhaps some nine to twelve months for most people who have lost a close loved one.

A person in this stage is not really happy, yet not angry or depressed about his situation either. He feels at peace with himself and the world, not just resigned to hopelessness. He reflects on the meaningful relationships he has had and on the deeper meanings of life and death.

During this stage of adaptation, recovery is in process. The person deals gracefully with realities he cannot change. He has been willing to face and overcome the pain caused by the loss. He works through it and then lets go. He is able to incorporate this grief experience into his conscious mind, acknowledging the reality and thereby reducing that intense pain.

The person finally realizes that life must go on. He has responsibilities. Emotional and practical adjustments must be made. Responsibilities in the family must be shifted to take up the slack left by the deceased loved one. The griever does not forget, but he deals with the great floods of emotional sorrow that block meaningful living. He begins to adjust emotionally to life, to fit in again. Yet the person at this stage is somewhat void of feeling. The griever is not bitter, not in severe emotional pain, but neither is he really living. He has merely adapted. There are increasing periods of tranquility and of hope for continued good life, however. There can be an increased reliance upon God to see him through.

I think of this stage as being more active than the acceptance stage of Kübler-Ross as she discusses acceptance of one's own death. In that case, one is rather passive, shows little interest in anything, and is often silent. He cuts himself off from others slowly and peacefully. He may merely want someone to hold his hand and reassure him. Adaptation, however, as I'm using the word, is active: one gets up, cooks breakfast, gets ready, goes to work, comes home, interacts with people, goes to church, repairs the car, changes the name on his bank account, probates the will, and just adapts to life again, though perhaps not enthusiastically.

The stage of adaptation may begin not too long after the death of a loved one, and it continues for many months depending upon how soon the griever faces his situation and works through it. Complete adjustment may never come, but one adapts. Although some grief may always be present, it is controlled. At the end of this stage, the person has fully accepted the loss and can affirm his own life.

One fact that helped me to accept Mom's death was my faith that she was going to a better place. Death is not always an enemy; it can sometimes be a friend. It brings us to another phase of life. "Whether we live or die, we are the Lord's" (Philippians 1:21). "Neither death nor life can separate us from the love of God" (Romans 8:31-39). Chaplain Coffin wrote in a recent article.

> But consider: if we are essentially spirit, not flesh; if what is substantial is not the other way around—then it makes sense that, just as musicians can abandon their instruments to find others elsewhere, so at death our spirits can leave our bodies and find other forms in which to make new music.[2]

What a beautiful illustration!

Mom's faith during her final days made acceptance of her death much easier. Her quotation of several Scriptures reminded us of her hope in something better. And as she continually struggled with her diseased heart, I wished for something better for her. So death brought a sense of relief as well as pain.

The stage of adaptation might be thought of as learning patience. Continue to work, continue to be patient, and life will get better. You have detached to some extent from the deceased and have adapted to your ongoing life. A relative sense of happiness that your deceased loved one would want you to have is not far away. Be patient. Do not feel guilty or disloyal, but reach for it.

Being forever unhappy is not a debt you owe your lost loved one. He would not want that. You do. But rethink it. What purpose would it serve for you to be unhappy forever? He wants you to go on with your life. As one widow said, "God gave me some more life. I'm going to have the courage to live it and to make the most of it. He would want it that way."

Reinvestment

The next stage of grief work might be called reinvestment. Adjusting is overcoming the negative, whereas reinvestment initiates the positive. This cannot be done well, however, until one has adjusted to, or come to terms with, the loss. A person cannot reinvest his interests in others until he has pulled away to some extent from the deceased. Then reinvesting in others takes place.

At this point, the griever has accepted the reality of the loss and is ready to rebuild his life. What is, is okay. One is satisfied with the promise of today and tomorrow.

The person expresses feelings and communicates normally. He reestablishes old friendships and makes new ones. He learns not only to face the loss, but to speak of it without reserve or shame as well.

The griever at this stage has learned to live with memories. Although holidays, birthdays, anniversaries, or other special days will still bring back moments of grief, he is more able to cope with the loss than he was before. Regressions are accepted and used as a creative rather than as a destructive force. As another writer says it, one has learned to say good-bye. Things will never be the same again, but one has adjusted.[3]

At this point, the bereaved is ready to enter into relationships with others. He participates with them rather than withdrawing. Earlier he did this in a forced way, but now he does it more naturally. He feels comfortable with his new identity. In all of this patience is required, since he may still feel at times as though he is taking one step forward and two backward, or two steps forward and one backward. So he takes his time. He needs to walk, not run, through recovery. He must work through grief with determination. Memories gradually become primarily a source of comfort rather than a cause of depression. Grief runs its painful, rebuilding, slow course. Its walls are gradually penetrated, and they begin to crumble. In all of this, a person is affected mentally, emotionally, physically, socially, and even spiritually. Yet a crushed life can be rebuilt in this process.

Various writers use different words to say that life for the griever should return to normal and then proceed with new friends and new interests. At the end of the stage of reinvestment, the person has fully accepted the loss, has learned to live without the deceased, and makes affirmation of his own life.

A person facing death himself usually hopes for either continued life or life beyond the grave. Such hope helps him to endure. Just so, hope in present and future life helps a griever not only to exist, but also to enjoy life again. Life has new meaning.

At the point of reinvestment, the griever has struggled with his new identity. Roles have been shifted in the family to "replace" to some extent the departed one. He realizes that he has lost a loved one but has not lost himself. He is a distinct person. He is still alive. As one reinvests energy into the lives of others, complete recovery begins as thoughts and habits become more attached to new objects and persons.

The griever's resilience and power enable him to find new meaning in life. There are tasks to be done, goals to reach, new patterns to establish, and new roles to play. Through grief work, he learns how to live again, to make the most of life, and to add life to his years, not just years to his life. There may also be a sense of restoration that takes place within the griever and his broken world.

Widows often feel that they have more difficulty in establishing new relationships than do widowers. They often have more difficulty with the establishment of a new identity. Mr. Jones is still Mr. Jones, but Mrs. Jones is not sure that she is still Mrs. Jones. "Mrs." expresses a relationship with a particular person, and he is dead. The widower also is more likely to have a vocational or professional life that helps in the maintenance of his identity. Mr. Jones is still a lawyer, a farmer, or an engineer. Although Mrs. Jones is not as likely to have a career, that is changing rapidly.

The widow's relationships with other family members, church friends, and other friends and acquaintances often take on a new and less-satisfying perspective. While others pity her, they also isolate her when she needs respect and assistance in her efforts to rejoin the community.

New meaning means new purpose. The griever needs to come to see that life is still worthwhile, that reinvestment is possible, that God is still interested in the bereaved and that others still need him.

Reinvestment may involve religion. How does one still relate to God? How has that changed? There are at least five spiritual responses one can make to the loss of a loved one: (1) this was God's will, and nothing else matters; (2) I don't believe, and nothing else matters; (3) I can incorporate death into an ongoing, vital faith and wrestle through the feelings with prayer and dialogue; (4) I can grieve the death within a belief system, or (5) I can plummet into a crisis of faith in which my old beliefs cannot accommodate death.[4] The third response would probably be ideal. The fifth might lead to a renewed faith and a renewed understanding of God's will that *can* accommodate to death.

One misconception some have is that it's wrong for a believer to grieve the loss of another believer. "After all, she has gone to a better place," we're told. I know from experience, however, that one still grieves such losses. Prayer, words of comfort, and Scripture readings may provide some comfort, but they do not remove the pain.

I have also seen numerous persons who feel a sense of guilt for grieving the loss of a believer: "I'm just being selfish," they say. Again, however, such grief is normal. Relationships may determine the nature of grief more than does religion, though religion is a vital aspect of grief work. Even Jesus wept (see John 11:35).

A person cannot reinvest in a normal way before he adjusts to the loss of a loved one. As he adjusts, energy and interest formerly attached to the deceased become available to reinvest in other people, other activities, and other things. This doesn't necessarily mean remarriage or new romance for the widow or widower. It does mean meaningful friends, good relationships, enjoyable activities, and a new interest in life generally. This goes a step beyond acceptance and mere adjustment in which the attitude is that one is alive and that's okay; life goes on. When one reaches reinvestment, it's good to be alive!

I have seen many people reinvest in life, and I salute them for it. They are courageous people who are willing to adjust and to reach out to others. They are not only survivors, but also conquerors. I hope you reach this stage. Keep working. It is out there somewhere within your grasp.

Growth

The last stage in the grieving process can be growth. I hesitate to list growth as a possibility in grief because grief is basically a negative, sad, and painful experience. Yet I list growth as the last stage of the grieving process because I have seen so many courageous people grow through grief; they came out of grief as more mature, stronger, and more well-rounded people than they were before the grieving experience began.

But how can something so positive come from something so negative? A welder welds a broken piece of metal together. The weld is so strong that it holds when other parts of the metal break. Thus, the welding process added strength to the metal.

A broken bone perhaps serves as a better illustration. The bone mends, and the mended spot is usually stronger than is any other spot on the bone. The break leads to a stronger bone.

Another illustration comes from the process of muscle building by means of weight lifting. All three of our sons were successful athletes: the shot put, the discus, the decathlon, football, and basketball. I learned a great deal about strength and weakness by watching them train. They ran, exercised, lifted weights, and practiced until they were extremely sore. In fact, after a good weight-lifting session, their muscles were torn down, broken, injured. But two days later, they were stronger and could lift more weight than before. The tear-down, rebuilding process made them stronger.

Something like this happens in the grieving process. One is torn down, but in the process he may grow stronger,

Table 1
Stages of Grief and How They Can Overlap

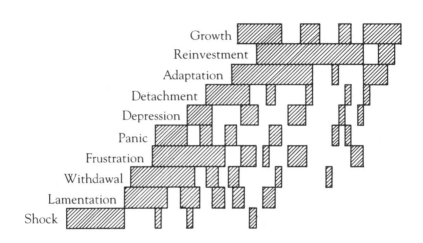

become more mature, and be more complete as a person than he was before.

As one reflects on the past, he becomes aware of his own mistakes: perhaps infidelity, loss of temper, excessive criticism, thoughtlessness, absence at the time of death, and other activities he now regrets. Some such regrets are universal. Such reflection, however, can lead to acceptance of that which cannot be changed, to forgiveness, and to improvement in behavior. Self-pity and guilt can be dead-end streets, but they also can be motivation for changed attitudes and actions. This is another way of saying that the person may grow through grief.

Stages are like roadmarks. They tell us about where we are on the road from the loss of a loved one to recovery. Everyone is different, so grief is different for each person. No two people experience the same recovery. It takes some longer than others to go through the process. Some may not experience every stage I have mentioned. Yet the vast majority of us eventually get through the process successfully, and many of us come out of it as better people than we were before.

6

GRIEF COUNSELING, PART I

Whether or not you're a professional counselor, at some point you will probably be around people who are grieving. If so, try to help. In this chapter and the next, I'll show you how. But as you read this, you may be a person who is still grieving yourself. In that case, I'd still recommend you read these chapters for several reasons.

First, by seeing my suggestions for counselors, you may gain additional insight into your own situation. Second, you may some day be in a position to help another griever—your own experience will give you valuable qualifications—and what you learn here could be extremely helpful to you then. And third, reading what a counselor should do, can aid you in choosing someone to counsel you in your time of need.

My advice on counseling the bereaved is organized around eleven verbs that summarize what a counselor needs to *do*. Those words are *care, learn, attend, control, listen, accept, wait, share, reinforce, innovate,* and *refer*. They are the keys to counseling that effectively help a bereaved person through the grief process.

When we try to help the grieving person, our goal is to help him face the loss, accept the reality of the situation, and readjust to life without experiencing a crippling reaction. The bereaved have seven primary needs: (1) support from others, (2) emancipation from the deceased, (3) acceptance of the pain of bereavement, (4) expression of sorrow and sense of loss, (5) verbalization of hostility and guilt, (6) formation of new relationships, and (7) finding meaning in life.[1]

A counselor may need to continue providing help in these areas for a year, two years, or even longer. This process goes far beyond the mere giving of advice and the sharing of comforting words: there is a sincere effort to help the griever confront his real feelings and work through them toward recovery, toward a sense of self-worth, and toward a lifestyle of happiness and usefulness.

Care

The effective grief counselor must love, must want what is best for those who grieve, must have the ability to feel with them, and must care. He may have healthy personality traits and varied intervention skills, but if he does not care about others, he will be ineffective as a grief counselor.

Such a caring person will show interest in the individual. No two people are alike. Each has a different background, character, personality, and spiritual nature. A counselor must try to understand the person before he can understand the problem. Then, the counselor can try to assess the situation.

Grief should not be an embarrassment. The bereaved should be encouraged to express, without interference, any honest and appropriate emotion he may be feeling.

Empathy is possible when one cares. A good counselor "feels with" the other person as he relives the experience.

He feels with the person through the expression of anger, pain, guilt feelings, and various memories of the past.

Empathy also identifies and clarifies the griever's deep feelings and conveys the perception that the counselor accepts the bereaved person's feelings as valid, without judging them. Judgment is suspended in order to fully understand what is going on in the life of the person. Such participation enables the counselor to learn many details of the death and to learn of other memories that have great meaning to the bereaved. But first, there must be genuine empathy.

As the bereaved person works through his grief, insight and understanding may result. Allowing *expression* of negative feelings can be helpful, but reinforcing them can prove harmful: it stifles the process of grief work. Since you care, show interest and encourage verbalization of feelings, even if the bereaved tells his story numerous times. Such verbalization helps him accept the reality of the experience. He comes to find some structure in what he's feeling.

When I first began our grief therapy groups, I often dreamed of experiences of our group members. I would see in my dreams coffins and scenes described in our groups. Although this stopped after a few weeks, I still will notice a few tears in my eyes from time to time as group members describe their sorrow. "I lost my husband to cancer, though he was just forty-six. My children are of no comfort to me. In fact, they add to my sorrow by their involvement in drugs and rebellion against me. Then last year I found out that I had cancer in my breast. I thought I could not take any more. It's so hard." Tears were not only in her eyes, but in mine also. I felt for her. I did care.

I have often spoken to groups of troubled people. On one occasion, a person who was dying of cancer said to me,

"What do you know about it? Are *you* dying of cancer?" I had to say that I was not, as far as I knew. I went on to say that while I didn't know exactly how he felt, I still cared. He seemed to accept that, and we went on from there.

My widow and widower friends accept me in the same way. They know that I don't know exactly how they feel—each of *them* is different—yet they believe I care. And they're right. Caring is an essential first step toward forming a counseling relationship that is therapeutic. If you find that you honestly don't care about others, work on yourself before you try to help them.

Learn

It is impossible to learn enough about grief to make it go away or to keep others from hurting. It always hurts when we lose someone we love, and it will hurt no matter how much our helpers know about grief. Yet certain beneficial knowledge is available. Such knowledge helps us not to make some mistakes that would be harmful to those who grieve, and that is very important.

As a beginning point, everything in this book up to this point could provide information for you. We learn from those who grieve. We learn from experience, and we learn from research.

Take a look at the stages I have discussed. Try to get an overall feel for those who grieve. Try to put yourself in their place. Learn and be reluctant to help: I mean by that, do not rush in with easy solutions. When people are hurting, they don't care what books say. Yet knowing how grievers feel may help *you* to be of help. You just sort of keep your knowledge in the back of your mind while you gently try to assist those who hurt.

Look at examples of those who grieve. Learn from them. Biblical examples teach a great deal about grief. Grief comes to all—even kings, even Jesus. Help is available. *Light* is seen at the end of the tunnel.

In addition to what I have already said about grief, I would like to highlight a few more specifics. Generally speaking, death may bring the deepest form of grief. There may be more shame connected with some divorce cases, with a child who has gone astray, or with imprisonment of a relative. Yet the pure grief caused by the death of a loved one may be even greater. Who knows for sure? Cases differ.

At any rate, grief from any source is difficult to handle. When one loses a spouse, he loses a partner, a confidant, a soul mate, a companion, a friend. After such a loss, almost everything will remind one of his deceased companion. The adjustment is difficult. Decisions are made differently. Relationships both new and old change. Every fiber of one's being is challenged by such a death. Coping requires every bit of one's strength.

Other losses also hurt: the death of a parent, the death of a grandparent, the death of a brother or sister, or the death of a good friend. A marital separation, a romantic breakup, losing an organ or a limb, an illness, deprivation of any kind, losing a job, being demoted, moving to another location, having a child leave home, abortion, the loss of personal property, or even retirement may cause grief. The pain of any kind of grief can be acute. In fact, I cried when our dog, Marvin, died. He had grown up with our boys. He was always a friend. He was always glad to see me even when I was grumpy. I thought about him for months after we had to put him to sleep. Of course, I would never tell anyone outside of my immediate family how much I was hurting because of the death of our pet dog. I even dreamed about him a few times.

From what people say, the death of a child is very difficult to handle. The timing is just not right. Parents are supposed to die before their children, we think. There is often guilt associated with a child's death, especially if he died because of genetic reasons. "It's my fault. I gave it to him," the parent surmises. One such parent said, "I will forever feel that this is the worst thing that can ever happen to you." There is even a high rate of divorce among couples suffering through the death of a child. Both parents are suffering acutely and seemingly cannot support each other at that time of great need. Such suffering and lack of support can create a great deal of hostility. Many women feel that their husbands are cold and uncaring because they grieve differently from the way they do.

You can learn much about helping others through grief by examining your own feelings about death, and especially the death of a child. Before it happens to you, take the time, one writer says, "to consider what a baby's death might mean to you. Examine your feelings at length and try to come to terms with them."[2] A counselor will be better prepared if he can reconcile the loss of a child with God's love, justice, and mercy before he gets into such a situation with someone he is trying to assist.

There are at least three reasons why grief by parents over the loss of a child is usually more intense and traumatic than are other types of grief:

> The tenacious emotional bonding between parent and child, the perception of the death as highly unnatural, and the perception among many bereaved parents that outside persons

60

in society often behave in ways that do not facilitate their grieving.[3]

An effective support person may be able to facilitate the grief process after the loss of a child and help parents work through their pain and anguish. Yet he cannot help unless he understands his own attitude toward death, toward the deceased, and toward the one who is grieving. Some have said that they adjusted to the idea of death by fantasizing their own death.

The counselor who has learned about the process of grief will realize that the griever has different needs at different stages of the grief process. He can then offer the help needed at each critical time. At first, the griever needs to face the fact of death. Then, there is a need to express the hurt openly and without shame, to talk of the past, the present, and the future. After two sessions of a G.R.O.W. group recently, one widow said, "I'm a lot better. I think it helped me to talk and cry it through. I can talk without crying now." Even verbalization of guilt, anger, and hostility can be therapeutic.

Then, there will be the need to withdraw at times and at other times to make friends. The counselor learns, listens, initiates, and responds. He does not try to fit anyone into a predetermined straitjacket. Each person grieves differently, and that is okay.

Grief reactions are defense mechanisms that allow the postponement of the full emotional impact of the loss, and they are generally normal reactions. Two illustrations of such mechanisms are *substitution* and *denial.* One substitutes an image or object for the loved one. Both love and hostility may be directed toward such substitutes. Denial may lead to perceptual and auditory disorders. One may have a sensation that the deceased is present or "hear his voice" or his footsteps in the other room.

These experiences are very common. Some of them can be explained in terms of conditioning psychology: a woman gets used to setting a place for her husband at the dinner table, so she continues to do so after he dies. She catches herself and stops. It's normal! She need not fear that something is wrong with her.

The degree of denial is affected by the nature of the death. If the death is untimely, denial is usually increased. The death is harder to believe. The young and the healthy are not supposed to die. Sudden death often causes severe reactions. In one study of twenty-three cases of *pathological* grief, the death was sudden in all twenty-three instances. The bereaved usually coped by blaming others.[4]

After a fatal nightclub fire, relatives of the deceased blamed the busboy who actually caused the fire when he attempted to replace a lightbulb, the person who removed the lightbulb as a joke, public officials who did not check the safety of the club's building, and the owner of the club for his lack of preventive action. These accusations seemingly have more substance than is often the case. I have heard widows blame themselves for not being able to make their husband go to a doctor. We are not to blame, however, for things we cannot control. And we are not superpeople, either. We are human and sometimes make mistakes.

Augustine, bishop of Hippo in A.D. 400, captured this feeling well. After his father's death, he spoke of his heart as "darkened by sorrow." His native place was a "torment" to him. His father's house represented "strange unhappiness." His memories of their experiences together turned into "cruel torture." He looked for him "on every side," but he was not there. He hated all things because they "no longer held him." He became a "riddle" unto himself: he could not understand why he was so sad and why "it afflicted me so grievously." No answer came. "Only weeping was sweet to me," he wrote, "and it succeeded to my friend in my soul's delight."[5]

In these lines from ages past, there is reflection of sadness because of losing a loved one, separation anxiety, and a strong desire to be together again. He valued his relationship with his father, so the loss was great. The very foundation of his life was shaken. He had lost part of himself, which resulted in pain and damage to his emotional life. He had become a part of his father. The death of his father meant partial death to himself.

But grief is more of a process than a state. The person moves on after withdrawing himself from the deceased. Redirection of attachment then takes place. All this is painful. The loss attacks the very meaning of his existence. His emotional investment must be redirected.

Notice that one's value system may be upset at the loss of a loved one. In fact, this often is the case. The person may not know what to believe anymore. If before a death one believes that God rewards those who are His, at the point of a loss such a person may conclude that "he is not His," that God has forsaken him. Yet if religion is ever to be meaningful, it should be meaningful at the point of death. And indeed, those with strong faith do find it to be a great comfort and guide in times of grief.

Belief in an afterlife often brings positive feelings to the bereaved, as well as belief in God's providential care, His love, and His provision of a future life for the one who grieves. Incorrect religious beliefs, on the other hand, cause letdowns during grief. An example might be a belief that if one lives right, God will never let anything unpleasant happen to him. At the death of a loved one, such a person will have to restructure his mental constructs of God. This is painful to do at any time, but especially during bereavement.

It's helpful to have some understanding of *abnormal* grief so you can recognize it and get professional assistance for the griever. Here are some symptoms to look for:

1. overactivity with a sense of loss.
2. the acquisition of symptoms belonging to the last illness of the deceased.
3. a recognized medical disease (psychosomatic conditions, colitis, rheumatoid arthritis).
4. alternation in relationships with friends and relatives.
5. hostility against specific persons.
6. schizophrenic symptoms.
7. lasting loss of patterns of social interaction.
8. coloring of activities detrimental to his social and economic existence.
9. agitated depression.[6]

Most of what we have been discussing is not abnormal grief. Abnormal grief comes from a fixation at one stage of the normal grief process. Grief is, thus, not worked through, and distortion of the normal grief process occurs. If a person is frozen in his grieving process for prolonged periods at any one stage, perhaps professional help is needed.

One can never learn everything about grief: people are so different, relationships vary greatly, and death comes in so many different ways. Yet some things can be learned, and they make a significant difference in our effectiveness in helping those who mourn. Knowledge about grief may at least help us not to hurt those who mourn, and that by itself is worthwhile. But perhaps we can move beyond not hurting them and actually be of positive help to them. That is my hope.

Attend

Being with someone who is grieving is unpleasant. It causes one to think of his own mortality. It brings sadness. Yet we will be very limited in our help if we aren't there.

I have often heard widows and widowers say that people sometimes say the wrong things to one who is grieving. A few examples are as follows: "You should be thankful that you had such a fine husband." "You had him for forty years. Mine died after only ten years of marriage." "Time will heal." "God does not make any mistakes." "You'll find someone else after a while." "You're not hurting like I am. He was my *son*. He was just your husband." 'If you really had faith, you would not grieve so much." "She is better off." The list could be extended greatly, but you get the idea. Those who grieve are usually offended by such statements as these. Sometimes, even at our best, we say the wrong things.

It almost always helps, however, just to be there—to attend, to honor the griever by our presence. A firm handshake, a helping hand with the chores—such help is almost always appreciated. One widow said, "My friend rushed right over when she heard. She said she was sorry and just sat there with me for a long time. I know she cared, that she hurt with me, that I could lean on her. Finally she got up, made some coffee, and picked up around the house. She helped me get through it all somehow. She knew just what to do and what to say. In fact, she didn't say much."

I have heard many people express similar sentiments. The pattern is the same: it's not so much what you say that matters as long as you don't say the wrong thing; it is *being* there and helping. Don't just ask if there is anything you can do. Think of specifics and do them: make the beds, help with funeral arrangements, make telephone calls, take the person to the funeral home and stay with him for a while, take care of the children, and just try to be a good friend. A touch, a facial expression, a tear, or a word that shows you are sharing his pain can be invaluable.

At this point, bereaved persons need support. You may be able to help when an immediate family member cannot. Be calm, be understanding, be supportive. Do not distort the reality of the situation. Accepting reality is the beginning step in the grief process. The sooner reality is faced by the griever, the less likely the grief will become pathological.

Jesus Christ is thought of by millions as "wonderful counselor" (Isaiah 9:6). He was concerned. He was empathic. He cried with his friends who had lost a brother. He came to be with them. His mere presence was helpful. And He asks us to be concerned also about those who suffer (see Matthew 25:35-40; John 11).

The apostle Paul admonished us to "rejoice with them that do rejoice, and weep with them that weep" (Romans 12:15). The Hebrew writer said, "Remember them that care in bonds, as bound with them; and them which suffer adversity, as being yourselves also in the body" (Hebrews 13:3).

Your presence with the griever may be needed for weeks, months, or even years. Be there. Encourage him to express his emotions and to talk about his loss if he wishes to do so. But primarily, just demonstrate concern by your presence for as long as it is needed.

When you are present, you may give attention to the expressed needs of the griever. The griever may just need you to sit there. He may need you to run errands. He may need you to listen as he describes the death, as he reviews details of the relationship. Perhaps just being a good friend, a good neighbor, or a caring person best sums up your role. Let the griever set the pace. But remember, the more the griever is out of control, the more the helper should take charge.

Control

Claud Lewis was a good friend of mine. He was like a second father to me at one point of my life. He served as an influential elder in the first church I served as minister. We named our third son after him.

When "brother Lewis" died of a sudden heart attack, the family asked me to "hold the funeral," which I was honored to do. Although I felt a lot of pain in my heart, I was able to preach the funeral without breaking down. But after the funeral was over, I walked out away from the crowd, broke down, and cried. I had stayed in control for the sake of others. I did not want to make their grief worse. I wanted to help them by paying just tribute to a good man who had gone on to be with the Lord. I did not want them to feel sorry for me.

Generally speaking, I don't encourage anyone who is grieving to hold emotions in for the sake of others, because it can hamper one's grief work. Mothers are good examples of this. A friend of mine said that she could not allow herself to break down at the funeral of her husband. She "had to hold up for the sake of our four children." But who knows? It might have *helped* the children if they had all cried together.

I don't think it is out of line for a minister or a psychologist to cry with people who are grieving. At least they'll know you care. One older church leader said, "People love a compassionate person, a person with a heart. You can't be all bad if you cry with people."

Yet there are times when one needs to stay in control. The situation is in turmoil. Everyone is coming apart. Somebody needs to be steady, to keep a level head, to be in control. In such a case, the counselor must not let himself "catch" the panic. He should give simple commands such as, "Let's just walk a bit" or "breathe deeply." The more out of control others are, the more in control the counselor must be.

I have noticed that it is helpful in my groups to show *some* compassion but not too much. I often feel a few tears rolling down my face as people describe their loss of a loved one. It just happens as I feel with them in their sorrow.

I think people appreciate such compassion. They can see that I care, that I am not merely doing my job. I doubt, however, that it would be helpful to them were I to allow myself to break down and cry. They would then feel sorry for *me* and try to help *me*. Yet I am there to help *them*. I want the attention to be on *them*. So, I try to maintain control even when I feel like breaking down and crying. I think this is the best professional approach to take: do not be afraid to feel, to care, but stay in control enough to keep the focus on *their* grief and not *yours*. If you care and if you stay in control, you should be able to help.

Listen

I'm not sure why, but it is very difficult to listen to those who are working through grief. Perhaps they make us think of our own death. We may think that their verbalization of sad feelings makes them worse. We may be threatened as helpers. *After all, we may reason, they sound so negative, and I'm supposed to help them feel better. If I could just get them to be quiet, then maybe I can still think of myself as an effective helper. What if they talk of suicide? I wouldn't know what to do.* There may be other reasons why we don't listen well. But whatever the reason, it is hard to hurt with people. I also know that we cannot help those who grieve if we don't listen and hurt a little with them.

My experiences with several hundred widows and widowers confirm this notion. They tell me that few people are willing to listen as they talk through their grief. "Maybe that's why I like to come to this group so much," they say. "You guys will listen." Almost every person in our groups has expressed this sort of feeling at one time or another. They need to work through their grief, but they are encouraged to put it behind them without talking much and without continued crying. They are left with a hard task with no means of accomplishing it. One might cry through grief or talk through grief, but it is very difficult merely to "put it behind you" without adequate expression of it.

We saw in Chapter 2 how "talking it out" helps the bereaved person. And in Chapters 3-5, we saw the stages through which a mourner passes and the grief work that needs to be done in each of them. The counselor's job is to facilitate that process by listening carefully, asking clarifying questions, reassuring the griever that his feelings are normal, and generally by helping the person to sort things out progressively and get on with life as he is able.

The expression of emotions can be encouraged by asking, "How do you feel?" Or you can say, "It might help to talk about it. I'll listen." "You look as if you need to cry" is also effective. I often tell those who grieve that crying helps, that crying proves that one is facing his grief, and that it takes a strong person to cry. And it does!

If you have difficulty in listening to a bereaved person, you might profit by asking yourself these questions:

1. Do I care about this person?
2. Am I personally threatened by the thought of death?
3. Am I afraid to listen for fear of being hurt?
4. Do I keep people at a distance as a defense mechanism?
5. Am I too busy to take time for others?
6. Why do I need to "fix this up" so fast?

There is a strange thing that often happens when real communication about one's grief takes place. One talks, and another listens, reflects, clarifies, questions, shares, and reinforces. Insight and understanding follow. Structure replaces chaos, and the mourner begins to recover.

One widow had not said anything for the first five weeks of her group. During the sixth session, she began to talk! Everyone else listened, reflected, empathized, and reinforced. After about ten minutes of talking, she had come to terms with her husband's death and had articulated plans for continued living. She later told me that she had "worked her way out of the woods" during that session.

When I first saw this sort of thing happen, I did not believe such a change could come about that easily, yet it did. After I saw it happen numerous times, I began to believe that something very important was happening in such sessions. And, after all, it wasn't easy, either. That widow had been coming to group sessions for six weeks. She had listened and cried. She had struggled until finally she was ready to talk it out.

If you're grieving, this can happen to you. If you're a counselor, allow yourself to help others. You may have more power as a person than you have ever imagined. Why not use it to assist others?

7

GRIEF COUNSELING, PART II

So far we've considered five of the eleven verbs that summarize the counselor's job when it comes to those who are grieving. And lest the job might start to sound like a huge, burdensome task, let me assure you it's not. You don't need a Ph.D., and you don't need to master all eleven functions before you can begin.

The most important requirement for being a good counselor is that you care for hurting people and that you are sensitive to the need of the moment. You can always come back and review this material as necessary, and that together with experience will help you become an increasingly effective counselor.

It's also true that I've known few more rewarding times than when a person has gone from the initial shock of bereavement, through counseling with me, to the growth and reinvestment in others that characterizes a healthy exit from the grief process.

With those thoughts to spur us on, let's return to our discussion of the eleven verbs that capsulize the counselor's job.

Accept

To help those who grieve, one must accept their pain as valid and accept them as persons of value. Otherwise, the one who hurts will not believe that you care or understand. Without such belief, he won't allow you to help.

Counselors with a strong sense of values or a rigid personality structure often have difficulty with acceptance. They see it as endorsement or agreement, but it is not. It is validation of the other person's experiences as being real. It is acceptance of another person as being of value as a person. It is not judgment of the person or his deceased loved one as being right or wrong, good or bad, lost or saved. Acceptance communicates care and concern for the other person. Jesus accepted the woman caught in the very act of adultery, even though He disagreed with her behavior (see John 8:3-11). We can accept another person even though he is of another race, another religion, or even if he has no religion at all. We can accept the poor, the uneducated, the uncultured. Their experiences are very real and extremely important to them. Their hearts beat just as ours do. We can learn to accept people and to help them work through their grief even though we don't agree with their beliefs or their behavior.

Ministers have often said to me, "But what if they think he went to heaven and you know he didn't? Aren't you going to tell them the truth?" This brings up a couple of interesting questions: (1) What purpose would it serve to tell them their loved one did not go to heaven? and (2) Why not let God be the judge? If a person wanted to know my understanding of salvation for his own benefit, I would gladly discuss that with him at the proper time and in the proper situation in order to help him, but not to judge his departed loved one. That is not my job. I am not qualified to do it anyway. There is always a good possibility that my list of the saved might be different from God's, and His is the only one that counts.

So, I accept each person as being of value. I stay out of the judging business. I concentrate upon the griever, his experiences, and what will help him. If he believes that I accept him, he can accept me as a helper. Perhaps then progress can be made.

Wait

I don't like to see people suffer. When they cry, I want to say something that will make them stop crying. When they ask hard questions, I want to give sure, helpful answers. It's hard for me to wait, to let them struggle, to see them cry, to go slowly; but it is very necessary to do this in dealing with grief. If you provide a quick fix, the fix doesn't last. So, I continually tell myself to wait. Let those who grieve take their time. Then, when they work through it at their own pace, the cure will last. There seldom is an easy answer to a hard question.

One tendency in our society is to postpone grief work by means of sedatives. "Let me give you a little sedative" is often the approach to grief by well-intentioned doctors. Many grievers resent this. Many have told me, "I didn't *want* a sedative. I wanted to *be* there, I wanted to *feel.* That's just putting it off. I don't want to rely on those things." In most cases, sedatives should be avoided when the purpose is to knock out the anxiety-mediating neural mechanisms. The main damage done by such medication is postponement of grief work until later, when it is actually more difficult to work through it. Give a person time to work through grief, but not by drugs. Do not rush in with answers. Learn to tolerate a little pain. Do not expect people to get over the death of a loved one quickly. Learn to wait.

Grief Counseling, Part II

Share

There are times in counseling when I just listen and reflect what the person is saying. And there are times when this may be all that's needed. The person is extremely upset and needs to talk. Yet after a while, even in such cases, counseling usually needs to go beyond mere listening and reflecting. The sharing of one's own thoughts, feelings, and concerns can sometimes be very helpful, too.

I usually begin a grief therapy group by introducing myself, explaining the group process, and giving a brief profile of my family and some grief experiences in my life. I then invite them, as they feel like doing so, to do the same, and they do. One at a time talks; the others listen and interact. They usually tell about their mate's sickness, long struggles in the hospital and at home, or the shock of a sudden death, the funeral, their children, their life together, and what it has been like since the death. Usually, everyone in the group says something during the first two-hour session. Sometimes one person remains silent, except in telling her name and a few brief remarks about her family. Within two or three sessions, everyone is usually talking, listening, and sharing solutions to struggles. In looking back at films of our sessions, I think my discussing a few personal experiences tells the others that it is okay to do the same.

By sharing, grievers help one another solve problems. One asks, "What do you do with your husband's clothes?"

Another answers, "It was hard for me to even look in his closet, but this is what I did. I got my daughter to come over and help me one day, and we went through everything he had, saved a few things we wanted to keep, and gave the rest away to a charity. I've felt better ever since. I needed to get them out of my sight so that I wouldn't have to see all his things every time I turned around."

That isn't a bad idea, is it? They have been through similar experiences, and they help each other. One says she doesn't know what to do with her wedding ring. Another says, "This is what I did. I wore mine for a few months. Then I decided that I was no longer married. So, I quit wearing it but had a jeweler make it into a nice pin that I now wear a lot. I still enjoy it but not as a wedding ring." Again, not a bad idea.

Notice that they aren't telling others they *must* do likewise. They are just sharing ideas.

One woman doesn't know what to call herself. Is she Mrs. John Doe, Mrs. Jane Doe, Ms. Jane Doe, or just Jane Doe? Another shares this idea, "I think it's up to each individual, but here is what I did. For a while, I was Mrs. John Doe. I just did not want anything to change. I was still his wife. Then, I ran into some legal problems and began putting everything into my name. Now I'm just Jane Doe. I'm not married anymore. It's not my fault. It's nothing to be ashamed of. It's okay."

I have seen this happen over and over again in our groups. Widows and widowers are there with many different time spans since their mates died. Each is different in many ways, and they have many different perspectives. As they share these, they help each other. They not only learn new ideas, but they also get "permission" to go on with their lives. They learn that it is quite okay to be happy.

In our groups, we have shared not only ideas, but also many other things: poems, family pictures, meaningful sympathy cards, helpful Scriptures, as well as other items. The pictures help them to talk about good times as well as bad times, to learn to deal with memories. They help us to know each other better and to be of more assistance to each other. We often end a group by going out to dinner together. And once each year, Memorial Park Cemetery and Funeral Home sponsors a nice Christmas luncheon for all who have been in a group. These are highlights of my year. So many courageous people are smiling, looking nice, and going on with their lives. A widow came up to me at our recent luncheon and said, "Remember me? I'm the one who cried all the time. But I'm doing fine now." Well, lots of people "cried all of the time," and that's okay.

I sometimes will tell a story to make a point. I might describe a dream I had after my mother died or how I questioned God's wisdom and love when my wife, Louise, had a serious attack of blood clots that went through her heart to her lungs. Grievers always seem to relate well to such stories. I tell how hard it was to deal with deep feelings. I never make it sound easy, because it isn't.

At other times I may tell a story about someone else. "I'm not sure if I could adjust as well as this widower did," I say. "It seems almost impossible, but I remember this one guy whose wife died suddenly. He was crushed and wanted to die himself. He was in shock for weeks. Finally, he began to see that she would want him to keep on living. He started getting up and going to work. He went back to church and just gradually regained his sense of purpose. He's doing well now."

You have to time these stories well and choose the right one, but some of them can be very helpful if not overdone. People are not as defensive about a story as they are about advice. Perhaps this is why Jesus spoke so often in parables.

One thought I have always shared is my belief that working through grief is not easy. It's very hard. Sometimes

I will just admit that I don't know answers to their questions. I may reply, "It's hard to know, isn't it?" or "I wish I knew."

I believe it is especially helpful for a counselor to share his thinking about false guilt feelings. Some 85 percent or more of the grievers I have worked with have had such feelings. "I feel guilty because I was not the wife I should have been" "I did not say good-bye to him before he died." "He died while we were having sex. It was my fault." "I didn't get him to the doctor in time. I should have taken him sooner." These and other such feelings are numerous. A discussion of them may be very helpful. You may be able to help relieve such feelings along these lines: "You did about what I would have done. You did what you knew to do at the time. It's easy to be a Monday morning quarterback." Such shared thoughts may make a great deal of difference in the minds and hearts of grievers.

What I am saying to you as a helper is that it's okay to share. Be genuine. Let yourself come through. In doing so, you may be of great help to those who mourn.

Reinforce

All of us have learned the value of reinforcement in everyday life. A child brings home a good report card, and we say, "Good job. You did well. I'm proud of you." He goes back to school and works harder. A husband comes home early from work. His wife greets him enthusiastically at the door with a big hug and kiss. He tries to get home early more often.

Reinforcement is a term that is closely associated with behavior modification and behavior therapy. Edward Thorndike was a pioneer in experimenting with the effects of

reinforcement on animals. Feeding was usually the rein-
forcer, and animals performed for food. B. F. Skinner has
amplified this principle. His emphasis is upon reinforcing the
behavior you wish to recur. That often is all it takes to shape
behavior in animals, and such research has been generalized
successfully to human beings. What reinforces one person
may discourage another, but behavior that is reinforced tends
to recur. Thus, behavior patterns are formed.

I often reinforce certain behavior in grief counseling:
feeling, thinking, and acting behavior. A widow says that
she is now able to talk about her deceased husband without
losing control.

"Good. That represents progress to me," I reply.

Another says, "Well, I finally started getting up in the
morning anyway. I ate breakfast several times this past week
and cleaned up the house. I think that's pretty good for me."

"It *is* good. I'm glad to hear that," I reply.

Another says, "I don't have much money, but I'm not
giving up, I'll look for a job."

"You know, you're pretty tough. I have a feeling you're
going to do all right," I answer.

She smiles and says, "I do too."

Still another tells of his struggles to take care of himself
since his wife died. He can't cook, he makes a mess out of
things around the house, he withdraws and clams up a lot. I
reply that I think he is doing well under the circumstances
and that I'm not sure I could do as well as he's doing. That's
the truth. He begins to feel as though he may be doing better
than he thought and is encouraged to keep trying. In group
counseling, others invariably join in and reinforce healthy
actions better than I do. It catches on and can be very
effective.

Reinforcement is a very necessary part of grief counseling. All counselors do it. We look, we nod, we smile, we command, we review progress. All of these are done at certain times and reinforce certain behaviors: feelings, thinking, and action. We choose what we reinforce. These choices are based upon our experiences and our values. We reinforce efforts to live rather than to commit suicide because we value life. We encourage interaction with people rather than withdrawing behavior because we deem interaction to be healthy. We encourage friendships, industry, and thinking because we believe these are signs of healthy living.

Everyone operates on some value system and reinforces behaviors he deems healthy. And there is so much difference between healthy and unhealthy behavior as it applies to grief that it's usually easy to detect which is which. The bereaved know the difference and usually don't argue with you. You are working toward agreed-upon goals. An exception to this principle might be a suicidal person. At that point, you work toward saving a life even though he is working toward death, because you believe life is best. Many times the person comes to agree with you at a later time. This has happened several times in our groups.

Proper reinforcement helps shape behavior. Used in a healthy way, it can be very powerful. It helps lift a griever up and move him forward during the entire grief process.

Innovate

When Jack Redden and I first talked about grief counseling, I had never used the group approach to counsel with such people. I had used it with divorced people briefly, and I had counseled with individuals and with families who were grieving, first as a minister and later as a counselor. I didn't know for sure how the group process would work with grievers, but I was willing to try. I had been in several groups during my graduate school training and had read extensively about group counseling. My experiences in groups led by Dr. Don Sime, Dr. Larry Bernard, and Dr. Maxine Bernard were helpful.

I began thinking of how these experiences and ideas could be adapted to help a person work through grief. We could get a homogeneous group. They would be able to talk and to express their emotions freely. They should empathize with each other, share helpful ideas, and reinforce each other. They should form a healthy, cohesive group. And they *did*, over and over again. This happened because we innovated over and over again.

Some professionals ask, "How do you know what caused the changes? Which part of what you did helped?" I really don't know. I also doubt that that's very important to the people who were helped. What part did the counselor play? the assignments? the other grievers? the setting? As in most field research, it's hard to isolate such variables. We just know that what we did was helpful to some five hundred grievers, and that it was very rewarding. That's where the rubber meets the road. There will be time later, perhaps, for others to try to further isolate possible variables that are helpful. But for now, let's talk about innovating.

We not only innovated by using the group method, but we also applied many tried and proven therapeutic tools to grief counseling. We talked, we listened, we empathized, we accepted clients, we understood, we interpreted, we reinforced, we made assignments—reading, changing actions, talking. We often taught progressive relaxation. We discussed dreams. I suppose that I have adapted every counseling method I normally utilize and used it in grief counseling. I encourage you to try this. Be creative. Be careful, but use the therapeutic tools you have learned. Change whatever you need to change. Counseling tools were made for people, not people for counseling tools.

Ministerial counselors, for example, often use Bible reading and prayer in their counseling. They could apply these to a group setting. In prayer a counselor can say things that he ordinarily would not be able to say. This gives the counselor more flexibility, and it can be very therapeutic.

Ministerial counselors should be better prepared than most to deal with certain types of problems. Guilt is an example. Real guilt calls for forgiveness, which points toward God. The griever is unable to correct past actions. There may have been infidelity, loss of temper, thoughtlessness, absence at the time of death, as well as many other problems. The griever cannot apologize to the deceased or correct past mistakes, so he punishes himself for all of these, often blowing them up into ever greater sins. But we all make mistakes, we are human, and we need forgiveness. This comes from God; thus, ministers should be able to help.

Guilt *feelings,* however, are different from guilt. Whereas guilt is objective, guilt feelings are subjective. Guilt corresponds to reality: guilt feelings may not. We may *feel* guilty and not really *be* guilty. Much of the guilt in grief is not guilt so much as guilt feelings. Of course, such feelings are very real to the griever, but any well-qualified counselor should be able to help such people toward clarification and forgiveness of self.

There are several specific ways Scripture may be used. Some passages speak of burdens and burden bearing. There are some burdens we must bear (see Galatians 6:5), some that others can help us bear (see Galatians 6:2), and still others that only God can bear (see Psalm 22). We are to cast those upon Him. Passages may be found on almost any topic or emotion. Such Scriptures may help not only by increasing understanding, but also as a springboard for further discussion. I have benefitted especially from 1 John 4:8; Philippians 4:4-9, 13, 19; and Romans 8:31-39. God is love; thus, He loves me and wants to help me. I can rejoice in the Lord and take all my anxieties to Him in prayer. I can cope in Christ. God is for me, so it should not matter who is against me. I continue to rely upon Psalm 23: "The Lord is my shepherd; I shall not want."

The minister may also use the biblical examples of grief mentioned earlier to encourage those who mourn. If King David and Jesus grieved, I should not expect to be exempt from grief. They worked through it, and so can I. As a counselor, do not push these ideas, just sort of imply them. When the griever is ready, he will take hold and move forward.

The minister has an advantage over other professionals in helping grievers. He is used in the funeral. He can visit homes, write letters, make phone calls, perhaps preach to them in church, or invite them over for dinner. Ministers can also make opportunities to utilize photographs, scrapbooks, family albums, mementos, and personal effects therapeutically. As the griever tells him about each item, he learns to deal with the various related memories.

The small group support method is especially suited to the church as well. The minister can arrange for such a group, provide space for their meetings, and call them together.

The minister can utilize many forces in addition to those already mentioned: the church library, worship, classes, the Bible, and others in the church, to name just a few. And there is spiritual support that transcends the counseling relationship. Ministers should take care, however, that Scripture is not used as an opiate or crutch that stifles therapeutic activity. Care should also be taken in using Scripture as prescriptions. For while the Bible can be used as a very helpful resource, it can also be misused.

The Psalms, which are excellent for grief counseling, typically reflect the important dimension of disorientation, of transition. In Psalm 23, one walks through the valley of the shadow of death; in Psalm 40, he is drawn from the miry bog. In Psalm 62, one is like a leaning wall or a tottering fence; in Psalm 90, the people are like grass that flourishes, fades and withers. Many of the Psalms give form to the worst experiences of life for Israel, and such expression leads them from distress to healing.

Another good idea is to recommend good books for the griever to read. It may help him understand what he's experiencing. Such reading can serve as a springboard for discussion in counseling. Since I have often utilized this method, I hope this book will be such a helpful source for many.

Role playing can be adapted and used in grief counseling. When one has difficulty in letting go of a loved one, he may be helped by speaking to an empty chair as though it were his deceased relative. He is encouraged to say the things he would say if the deceased were present. This may be especially helpful in sudden, unexpected, and untimely deaths.

I've also used role playing by sitting in for the deceased. I have the mourner say to me what he would like to say to the deceased. Then, I often say to him what I think the deceased would say. The experience is often so real that people comment afterward that they're glad "I got that settled." And they did. They worked through it as the deceased would want them to do.

There are many other methods that could be adapted and used in grief counseling. Imagery is a good illustration. Even hypnosis could be helpful if used wisely by a well-trained therapist. My suggestion is to utilize the tools that are familiar to you. With a bit of innovation, any counseling method might be adapted and used in grief counseling.

Discussion of the bereaved person's dreams may also be helpful. Dreams are an important growth process in which the subconscious mind gradually places the reality of the death into the conscious mind. As the person dreams, he gradually works through his grief. The subconscious mind uses one's experiences as a background and tells a story that depicts the current emotional state of the griever. And as the person tells his dreams, he gains insights and is able to go on toward recovery. To facilitate discussion, the counselor might describe some of his own dreams with grievers, as I've done.

An example might help clarify. Right before I went back home for my family's first Thanksgiving Day reunion, after Mom's death, I dreamed that I was trying to get to the old home place, but the road was blocked. Houses and apartments had been built in the road. The message "It's going to be difficult to go back home" came through loud and clear to me. Perhaps that dream helped me to work through some subconscious materials. I did return home and am glad I did. Dad's new wife is a fine woman. She was very gracious to all of us. Yet right after I returned to my own home, I dreamed that I was back at the old family home, sitting in the swing on the porch, at a family gathering. Mom came walking across the porch. I was excited but also afraid to show excitement, because I knew that Dad was remarried and felt that the family was sort of shaming me for being excited to see Mom. I was also thinking in the dream, *Dad can't be excited, because Mom's being here makes him a bigamist.* You see, all of my emotions have not been straightened out yet. It will take some more time. But I see progress reflected in my dreams, and I am trying to work through some complicated feelings.

In grief counseling as in other counseling, the counselor encourages the individual to utilize every source of strength and help available: the person's own inner resources, children, friends, extended family, people in the church, the minister, and various resources in the community. Such resources may help a griever adjust and again become a vital working part of society.

When one person dies, it isn't just one family member who is affected but the entire family. When a parent dies, the whole family is hurt and needs to be helped. The children must not be overlooked, as they often are. Everyone is to be considered. This is true even when individual counseling is being done. The individual is viewed as being a part of a family. Grandchildren often hurt a great deal at the death of their grandparents. The one closest to the deceased may need more help, but others should not be ignored.

Refer

No matter how well-trained and experienced a counselor might be, he will need to refer people to other counselors at times. Someone else may be better qualified, or clients may not be making much progress. Refer if you need to do so. Don't take your inability to help a particular individual as a personal failure.

If you have any question about whether a referral should be made, your wisest course is to go ahead and make it. The old adage "Better safe than sorry" certainly applies here. Refer back to Chapter 6 under *Learn* for information about common symptoms of abnormal grief, and be prepared to make appropriate referrals as necessary. People who need more help than you can give deserve to be referred to a professional who can give that help. They may suffer for a lifetime without it.

I have used eleven verbs to organize my thoughts on grief counseling. If you want to help people in this way, you would do well to engage in all these actions: care, learn, attend, control, listen, accept, wait, share, reinforce, innovate, and, perhaps, refer. I pray you'll have a fruitful experience as you try to aid others.

8

THE GRIEF RECOVERY GROUP

"Many thanks for allowing me to speak out." "Thank you for letting us pour out our hearts. I hope other funeral homes and even churches will help people to talk it out. It's great!" "I'm the one who talked about jumping off the bridge. Well, I'm glad I didn't now. My life has really changed. I'm married again, and it's great! Thanks for not giving up on me."

These and many similar comments have come to Jack Redden and me from people who have taken part in our Grief Recovery of Widowed groups. Such remarks bear witness to the effectiveness of this method in helping bereaved people move through the grief process more easily and quickly. I've seen over and over how much this group experience can mean to mourners, and I strongly encourage you to get involved in one if it's available, or to help get one started if there isn't one where you live.

I have already discussed at some length and in several places the many benefits that come from these groups, so I won't list them all again at this point. Three of the primary benefits, however, are that (1) they get grieving people talking about their feelings; (2) they bring about lots of good sharing between people who are suffering in the same way and who can, therefore, offer one another excellent insights;

and (3) they help people see that their grief experience is normal.

In follow-up research done by Jack Redden and myself, we have found that the group experience generally helps people improve faster than they would if left on their own to deal with their grief. This improvement shows up in several important categories: level of grief, expression of feelings, extent of social relationships, and feelings about the future, to name just a few.

In addition to conversation about experiences and feelings, a typical group meeting may include the sharing of family photos, Scriptures, poems, and other things that have proved meaningful or helpful to group members. And once a year we hold a banquet for all who have been part of a group in the preceding twelve months. That's always one of the highlights of my year.

Although the average age of participants in our groups has been fifty-nine, ages have ranged from as young as twenty-nine to as old as eighty-one, and the experience has been good for them all. The people have been widowed an average of thirteen months, but here, too, the range is quite wide: from just a few days to as long as eight years. And once again, virtually all of them have benefitted from their participation.

Getting Started

Clearly, a group made up of widowed people—or any group of grieving people—has to be put together by someone with access to lists of such people. Logical candidates are ministers, counselors, doctors, and funeral home directors.

If you're looking for a group or would like to help get one started, these are the kinds of people you should approach.

For a group meeting to be effective, it also needs to be run by a professional counselor who can keep it on track. Without a trained and fairly objective person there to keep the meeting moving ahead, it can get mired down in negatives and pity. As noted earlier, any counseling meeting should accept negative feelings but not create or reinforce them.

I've found the ideal group size to be about ten. And groups typically meet once a week for two hours over a period of six to eight weeks. That time frame seems to work out well. It's long enough to get some grief work done, but not so long as to become burdensome.

With those thoughts as background, let's look now at an excerpt from the transcript of a grief recovery group's meeting. It will give you a first-hand review of how such a group functions. Please note that names and some details have been changed to protect the anonymity of the individuals involved. And notice how the participants ask questions, share insights and encourage and support one another.

The Group Meeting

Lucy: I don't know whether this is out of line or not. There are several widows in my Sunday school class. I taught Sunday school there for fourteen years before Tim got too sick, and I think there was just one widow at that time. Some more came in. Two or three had lost their husbands. But they are the most precious human beings I've ever been around in my life, and they sit at home and cry and they're afraid to drive their cars. Even after four or five years, they're scared to drive a car. They won't get on the expressway. They wouldn't come out here to Poplar. They won't drive to this place and that place to eat. They won't go any place, and they tried to corral me into their grief. But I'm not going to do that. That doesn't mean I don't cry, because I do.

Bill: One thing you have to try to guard against is withdrawing from life. That's what you feel like doing.

Lucy: Well, that's what several of these women have done. Now one does work part-time, and she's not very well physically. But the others just sat down and started feeling sorry for themselves.

Bill: You've been going here for what, ten years or so with all this? Since the first heart attack?

Lucy: Twelve and a half.

Bill: Twelve and a half years!

Jean: Fantastic!

Bill: Wow!

Lucy: I worked all that time.

Margaret: You're a marvelous person.

Lucy: 'Til, uh. . . .

Jean: Were you in good health?

Lucy: No. I've got a lot of ailments. Not in good health, and in August I struggled on. He had surgery in May, and I struggled 'til August to do my job, just going in and working the payroll and doing emergency things. I knew in July that I had to keep it up, so I had to work part-time. But it gave me something to do.

Bill: A lot of times after a person has a heart attack he will be very depressed.

Lucy: He was very depressed. *Very* depressed.

Bill: It's sort of a common thing. It's almost like you die. He got so close to dying, you know.

Lucy: It scared me to death!

Bill: You just run scared all the time, having to live with that dread. You know—go ahead.

Lucy: And their disposition is bad too.

Bill: Yes, their dispositions may change. It's almost like they are a different personality. And another thing is the extreme pain that he went through. Obviously the kind of pain you were talking about can cause many unusual reactions.

Lucy: Well, he was a strong person. He had a strong will and a strong body.

Bill: Well, we appreciate your sharing that with us. It's hard to talk about so many things that hurt so much.

Lucy: Well, I have found that the husbands of my friends—of course, I have a lot of Sunday school friends because I taught for a number of years and got real close to all of the people that I taught. All of them haven't kept in touch with me, but a great many have, and I have found the husbands giving me attention helped me. We went to a Christmas party, and I knew that that was really going to be hard for me. When I got to the Christmas party, I was the belle of the ball because they went all out to be nice to me, to do this for me and that for me, and to tease me and say nice things about me and also. . . .

Bill: Yeah.

Lucy: That's just normal things, and they invited me out and took me out for dinner one night. Then one of the ladies in the Sunday school class had

a luncheon before Christmas. They had wanted
to come over to my house, and I said, "No, I
don't want to be bothered with you." Well,
with an answer like that most people would just
turn around and leave you alone. But they
haven't. They have kept—

Margaret: Well, I can see why they'd want to be around
you. (Laughter.)

Bill: You know, I think it's a shame in our society
that usually when a man says something to a
woman it is interpreted by a lot of people as
though he's interested in sex, just automatically.
You need friends who are women, and you need
friends who are men, you know, without
anything being wrong with it.

Jean: I think you need men to talk to. I think men
have a different outlook on life, and a lot of
women need men to converse with.

Lucy: To get a different point of view of life.

Bill: Yeah.

Jean: That's what women need in men, even though
they are not looking for sex.

Bill: Right. I think that probably helps explain why
you don't have as many men friends, like you're
afraid the wives will misinterpret it or, you
know, something like that.

Lucy: Well, I think I'm fortunate really, and last night
we were at this prayer meeting. One of the wives
said, "Are you going to let my husband make a
garden in your backyard?" And I said, "Well,
are you going to come over with him every time
he works the garden?" She said, "Well,
certainly not." I said, "Well, what will the
neighbors say?" (Laughs.) And she got really

amused. So she had to tell it, and they had a big laugh about it.

Bill: Dot, how long has it been since your husband died?

Dot: (Cries.)

Bill: It really hurts, doesn't it? We all understand that.

Ann: She's got a whole different set of problems.

Bill: Yeah. You know, one thing that really amazes me is that I've worked indirectly with this sort of thing for twenty years, and I thought I'd heard all kinds of situations. But I never had heard anything like what you've told us today before in my life, not exactly like that.

Lucy: I've never heard anybody survive that much.

Bill: No, never. And Joy there; nobody else can look at you and say, "I know exactly how you feel."

Jean: You know I never did tell you—I just told you my husband was killed in a traffic accident, but several years before he was killed in a traffic accident. . . . We have a swimming pool, and he broke his neck in the swimming pool.

Bill: I'll say.

Woman: Good gracious!

Jean: I had just quit work at that time, but I went back to work because I didn't know whether he was going to be confined for quite some time. It was very fortunate. He got over it. He wasn't killed in the traffic accident; but when I got to the hospital, the doctor told me that he was going to die, and my first thought was for him. . . . He could never be a vegetable. So, I remember I didn't cry. All I did was beg that doctor not to let the respirator go. I was so ignorant. I didn't know that when your heart stops, the respirator stops. His mind was very clear, but he could not speak. All he could do was blink his eyes and move his head from side to side and . . . but, that was the thing that struck me, to think of his comfort for the few remaining days that he had left. And I remember that.

Lucy: You know, this week is the first time I can remember that I've slept for a night without hearing my husband calling me. He was always up, and I would sleep with one ear open.

Bill: You got used to his being dependent on you. You've been conditioned over so many years, and that's just a part of your subconscious or something.

Lucy: It's a pattern.

Bill: It's a pattern. You get used to getting up at seven every morning. You sort of wake up.

Jean: You think of certain things you should do at certain times of the day. You just get accustomed to those things. To me, I could almost read my husband's mind. He would say the same things, think the same things. You're just together so much.

Bill: Just don't get shook and think something is wrong. You can't forget that fast.

Jean: Like they say, I never did have a guilty feeling after my husband died. Of course, he died so quick. Maybe that's the reason.

Lucy: I don't have a guilty feeling.

Jean: Don't you?

Lucy: I just wish I could tell him one more time I loved him.

Bill: He knew that.

Lucy: I was so tired that I felt like somebody could cut my head off and I couldn't feel it. Well, I have a strong faith. I didn't have that faith when my son was killed. I went to Sunday school spasmodically, mostly to take him when he was young. I would stay at home doing housework and working in the yard because my husband spent a career having fun. (Laughs.) He was down on the river, hunting and fishing, and all that kind of thing for three or four days, and building boats, and he was just busy from five in the morning 'til late at night. After Timmy was killed, I got a little better in a year. Tim got worse, and then he was not able to work for three years; but he built boats, and he just turned our back yard and garage into a boat factory, and he built two big cruisers and numerous just ordinary fishing boats. So I know that he had about as much fun as any human being could get out of life. I just haven't felt guilty at all.

Jean: Well, now, I have those thoughts, too. I wish I could see him and talk to him again, but that's not to be. You have to get over that feeling. I mean, that's how I feel about it personally. You must get over that feeling! He's never going to be there again.

Lucy: How do you get over those feelings?

Jean: You don't. You don't.

Lucy: You cannot say, "I won't think about this, I won't think about that." The only thing that you can do for the feelings that you have over grief is to give your time to something else, and that automatically pushes your—

Jean: Your feelings aside. I mean, that's how I feel about it. Now when I was here last week, I was a little depressed. After I got to talking to the people, I feel so much better because I can talk it out with somebody.

Bill: Well, good.

Jean: I know you all feel the same way as I do, even you. I know you feel the same way we do.

Bill: You get to where when it comes up in your mind, it just doesn't bother you as much. Just talking it out . . .

Jean: That's right.

Bill: . . . helps when you get to where you can do that sometimes.

Jean: It takes you a while to get to that point.

Bill: Oh, yes.

Ann: At first, you just can't talk about it at all.

Jean: No. It just takes a while. I know that this summer I took a vacation with my children, but when I came home it was lonesome.

Lucy: Well, will there ever be a time when you're not lonesome, and even when your husband was living, weren't there times when you were lonely?

Jean: Yes.

Bill: Yes. You'll get that way.

Jean: Yes. I've sometimes felt that way. You've just got to find new friends and make a new life for yourself.

Lucy: Well, I'm going to drop in on you some day and. . . .

Jean: I'll be glad for you to.

Lucy: Is it better to find friends like you are, in the same condition, or is it better to find friends to pull you out of the doldrums?

Bill: I believe you can have some of both. Friends like you are can help you because you feel like they can understand your feelings maybe in a way that others just don't.

Ann: You can help them, and that gives you a feeling of satisfaction. You can make them a little less lonely.

Jean: Well, I went to dinner with a couple last night. She works for the Red Cross. I'm going to take one of these Red Cross courses on first aid which she said would be very interesting. I'd just finished redecorating the house when my husband died. That left me with nothing to do, because I was busy working and raising my son, and, you know, just one thing after another.

Bill: I believe you're making some real progress.

Jean: Do you?

Bill: Yeah, I do.

Jean: Oh, well, I thank you.

Bill: It's a new life. You know, it's hard but—

Jean: You've *got* to make a new life for yourself!

Bill: You just think of the alternatives, that's just really—

Jean: I've got to meet new friends.

Bill: A widow in another group said you have to think of what you *do* have rather than what you *don't* have because the "don't have" thing is just a dead-end street.

Jean: I feel that what's in the past is in the past. I've got to look to the future because I don't have that many more years to live.

Bill: The memories are there and they add—

Jean: That's right!

Bill: They enrich your existence because they exist.

98

Jean: And I'll tell you another thing I found out. Since my husband died in an accident, I have had to hire a lawyer to handle my case. And I have found out that I am going to prepare for my son so that he will not have as many problems as I had when my husband died, you know, to take care of. And I am informing my own child of benefits he's entitled to so he'll know.

Bill: It's about time to go. You'll come back won't you? Okay. Bye, bye.

9

YOU CAN GROW THROUGH GRIEF

If you're a person struggling with grief right now, hang in there! There's a brighter future for you, full of life and hope. Based on my own experience and the experience of hundreds of people in our grief recovery groups, I know you're going through a hard, painful time. I think I understand something of what you're feeling, and it's okay. But I also know this can be a tremendous growing time for you, and you can come out of it a stronger person than you were before.

Reread the material on the stages of grief in this book several times. Use it to get a handle on what's happening in your life. Understand that whatever you're feeling or doing, it's probably fairly normal. Realize, too, that it's natural for the grief process to take some time to work out in your life. Quick and easy answers don't usually help. So give yourself time. Be kind to yourself.

If you're not already talking regularly with a caring, accepting person along the lines discussed in Chapter 2, I urge you to find such a helper soon. It can be an individual, or it can be a group of supportive people like the grief recovery groups in which I've been involved. But either way, finding a trustworthy person with whom you can talk it out is vital.

Bear in mind, too, that the pain of grief is usually worst right before we make progress in our grief work. As the old saying goes, "It's always darkest just before the dawn." So if you find yourself in a particularly dark time right now, perhaps it means some real progress is just around the corner. Keep looking for that light! The future is bright in spite of the present gloom; hang on to that truth.

It may be that right now you're beginning to find some happiness in life again, and that you feel guilty about it. This, again, is a common experience. However, think of it this way: If your deceased loved one were able to talk to you, what would he want you to do? Would he want you to be sad the rest of your life, or would he want you to find enjoyment in living again? If the positions were reversed, wouldn't you want your loved one to get on with life after a while and be happy again? As Ecclesiastes 3:4 tells us, there will always be "a time to weep, and a time to laugh; a time to mourn, and a time to dance."

If you're reading this out of a desire to help others who are grieving, I applaud your wish to help. You can make a tremendous difference in someone's life. You also should reread the chapters that will familiarize you with the grief process. Reread, too, the counseling chapters so you'll get some idea of what to say and, more importantly, do—and what *not* to say and do for a grieving individual.

Finally, I ask you to consider your relationship with God. He loves you and wants you to be His child, and He gave His Son's life to make that possible (see John 3:16). The Lord is a very constructive force in my life, and He can be in yours as well. He gives me cleansing from sins (see 1 John 1:7,9), strength to live (see Phil. 4:13; Isa. 40:28-31), and a sure hope (see 1 Pet. 1:3-4). We who are His will live forever with Him (see 1 Cor. 15; Phil. 1:21-23).

I hope you have been helped by the material in this book. I want to help and not to hurt. I do not criticize how you are grieving because I might do worse. I offer these ideas and feelings with a prayer that you will hurt less, that you will be able to go on with your life, and that you will be happy again.

BIBLIOGRAPHY

Alexy, William D. "Dimensions of Psychological Counseling That Facilitate the Grieving Process of Bereaved Parents." *Journal of Counseling Psychology* 29 (September 1982):498-507.

American Heritage Dictionary, 1983 ed. s.v. "grief."

Are, Thomas L. "Avoiding the Credit Trap." *Ministry.* (January 1983):4-6.

Augustine. *The Confessions of St. Augustine.* Translated by John K. Ryan. Garden City, N.Y.: Doubleday & Co., 1960.

Autton, Norman. *The Pastoral Care of the Bereaved.* London: S.P.C.K. Holy Trinity Church, 1967.

Avinoam, Reuben, and Sachs, H. *Compendius Hebrew-English Dictionary.* Edited by M. H. Segal. Tel-Aviv, Israel: Dvir Publishing Co., n.d.

Bachmann, C. Charles. *Ministering to the Grief Sufferer.* Englewood Cliffs, N.J.: Prentice-Hall, 1964.

Bailey, Robert W. *Ministering to the Grieving.* Grand Rapids, Mich.: Zondervan Publishing House, 1980.

Bayly, Joseph. *The Last Thing We Talk About.* Elgin, Ill.: David C. Cook Publishing Co., 1973.

Bonnell, George C. "The Pastor's Role in Counseling the Bereaved." *Pastoral Psychology* 22 (February 1971):27-36.

Bowlby, John. "Processes of Mourning." *International Journal of Psycho-Analysis* 42 (1961):333-38.

_____. "Separation Anxiety." *International Journal of Psychoanalysis* 41 (1960):89-113.

Brown, Larry T., and Weiner, Elliot A. *Introduction to Psychology.* Cambridge, Mass.: Winthrop Publishers, 1979.

Brueggemann, Walter. "The Formfulness of Grief." *Interpretation* 31 (July 1977):263-75.

Capps, Donald. *Biblical Approaches to Pastoral Counseling.* Philadelphia: Westminster Press, 1981.

Carr, Arthur C. "A Lifetime of Preparation for Bereavement." In *But Not to Lose: A Book of Comfort for Those Bereaved,* pp. 134-36. Edited by Austin H. Kutscher. New York: Frederick Fell, 1969.

Carrington, William L. "First Aid in Counseling: I. The Bereaved." *The Expository Times* 77 (November 1975):40-44.

Clinebell, Howard J., Jr. *Basic Types of Pastoral Counseling.* Nashville: Abingdon Press, 1966.

_____. *The People Dynamic.* New York: Harper & Row, 1972.

Coffin, William S. "Death: More Friend Than Foe." *The Christian Ministry* 6 (May 1985):5-6.

Coleman, James C., and Hammen, Constance L. *Contemporary Psychology and Effective Behavior.* Glenview, Ill.: Scott, Foresman & Co., 1974.

Collins, Gary R. *Christian Counseling: A Comprehensive Guide.* Waco, Tex.: Word Books, 1980.

Corazzini, John G. "The Theory and Practice of Loss Therapy." In *Bereavement Counseling: A Multidisciplinary Handbook,* pp. 71-85. Edited by Bernard Schoenberg. Westport, Conn.: Greenwood Press, 1980.

Dixon, Elizabeth N. "When Birth Means Death." *Christian Ministry* 15 (July 1984):16-19.

Bibliography

Edgar, Robert. "How to Understand Grief." In *Religion and Bereavement*, pp. 105-9. Edited by Austin H. Kutscher and Lillian G. Kutscher. New York: Health Sciences Publishing, 1972.

Farmer, Patrick J. "Bereavement Counseling." *Journal of Pastoral Counseling* 15 (Fall-Winter 1980):28-33.

Fischhoff, Joseph, and O'Brien, N. "After the Child Dies." *The Journal of Pediatrics* 88 (January 1976):140-56.

Flatt, Bill W. *Mental Health and the Bible.* Memphis: Christian Counseling Publications, 1979.

Freese, Arthur. *Help for Your Grief.* New York: Schocken Books, 1977.

Freud, Sigmund. "Mourning and Melancholia." In *Collected Papers*, 4:152-70. 5 vols. Edited and translated by Joan Riviere. New York: Basic Books. 1959.

Friedrich, Otto. "The American Way of Debt." *Time* (May 31, 1982):46-49.

Gerson, Gary S. "The Psychology of Grief and Mourning in Judaism." *Journal of Religion and Health* 16 (October 1977):260-74.

Goldberg, Jacob. "Issues in Pastoral Bereavement Counseling." *Journal of Pastoral Counseling* 15 (Fall-Winter 1980):5-18.

Goldfine, Marvin. "Accepting the Fact. In *Religion and Bereavement*, p. 115. Edited by Austin H. Kutscher and Lillian G. Kutscher. New York: Health Sciences Publishing, 1972.

Greer, Ira May. "Grief Must Be Faced." *The Christian Century* 62 (February 1945):269-71.

Grollman, Earl A. *Living When a Loved One Has Died.* Boston: Beacon Press, 1977.

Hare-Mustin, Rachel T. "Family Therapy Following the Death of a Child." *Journal of Marital and Family Therapy* 5 (April 1979):51-59.

Hecht, Manfred H. "Dynamics of Bereavement." *Journal of Religion and Health* 10 (October 1971):359-72.

Hiltner, Seward. *Pastoral Counseling.* New York: Abingdon-Cokesbury Press, 1949.

Hodge, James R. "They That Mourn." *Journal of Religion and Health* 2 (July 1972):229-40.

The Holy Bible; American Standard Version. Nashville: Thomas Nelson Publishers, 1901, 1929.

The Holy Bible; King James Version. Cleveland: World Publishing Co., n.d.

Hulme, William E. *Pastoral Care and Counseling.* Minneapolis: Augsburg Publishing House, 1981.

Jackson, Edgar N. *Coping with the Crises in Your Life.* 2nd ed. New York: Jason Aronson, 1983.

_____. "The Importance of Understanding Grief." In *Religion and Bereavement,* pp. 3-6. Edited by Austin H. Kutscher and Lillian G. Kutscher. New York: Health Sciences Publishing, 1972.

_____. *The Many Faces of Grief.* Nashville: Abingdon Press, 1972.

_____. *Understanding Grief.* New York: Abingdon Press, 1957; Nashville: Abingdon Press, 1959.

_____. *When Someone Dies.* Philadelphia: Fortress Press, 1971.

_____. "Why You Should Understand Grief: A Minister's Views." In *But Not to Lose,* pp. 45-49. Edited by Austin H. Kutscher. New York: Frederick Fell, 1969.

_____. *You and Your Grief.* Manhassett, N.Y.: Channel Press, 1962.

Jernigan, Homer J. "Bringing Together Psychology and Theology: Reflections on Ministry to the Bereaved." *The Journal of Pastoral Care* 30 (June 1976):88-102.

Keikkinen, Charles H. "Counseling for Personal Loss." *Personnel and Guidance Journal* (September 1979):46-51.

Kennedy, Eugene. *On Becoming a Counselor.* New York: Continuum, 1977.

Kidorf, Irwin W. "Jewish Tradition and the Freudian Theory of Mourning." *Journal of Religion and Health* 2 (April 1963):248-52.

Kisner, Jeffrey A. "A Family Systems Approach to Grief." *Pastoral Psychology* 28 (Summer 1980):265-76.

Kreis, Bernadine, and Pattie, Alice. *Up from Grief.* New York: Seabury Press, 1969.

Kübler-Ross, Elizabeth. "Anger before Death." *Nursing* 1 (August 1973):12-14.

_____. "Life and Death's Lessons from the Dying." In *To Love and to Die,* pp. 158-62. Edited by Robert H. Williams, New York: Springer-Verlag, New York, 1973.

_____. *On Death and Dying.* New York: Macmillan Publishing Co., 1969.

Leet, Don R., and Driggers, Joann. *Economic Decisions for Consumers.* Belmont, Cal.: Wadsworth Publishing, 1983.

LeShan, Eda. *Learning to Say Good-by.* New York: Hawthorn Books, 1976.

Lewis, C. S. *A Grief Observed.* New York: Seabury Press, 1961.

Liebman, Joshua Loth. *Peace of Mind.* New York: Simon & Schuster, 1946.

Lindemann, Erich. "Grief and Grief Management: Some Reflections." *The Journal of Pastoral Care* 30 (September 1976):198-207.

_____. "Symptomatology and Management of Acute Grief." *American Journal of Psychiatry* 101

(1944):141-47; *Pastoral Psychology* 14 (September 1963) :8-18.

─────────. "Symptomatology and Management of Acute Grief." In *Crisis Intervention*, pp. 7-21. Edited by Howard J. Parad. New York: Family Services Association of America, 1965.

McCullough, William B. "From Two Vantages: A Physician-Minister's Views." In *But Not to Lose*, pp. 26-32. Edited by Austin Kutscher. New York: Frederick Fell, 1969.

MacInnis, Helen P. "When a Child Dies." *Christian Ministry* 10 (January 1979):30-34.

Matz, Milton. "Judaism and Bereavement." *Journal of Religion and Health* 3 (July 1964):345-52.

Miller, William A. *When Going to Pieces Holds You Together.* Minneapolis, Augsburg Publishing House, 1976.

Moody, John H. "Dreaming and Bereavement." *Pastoral Psychology* 26 (Fall 1977):12-22.

Morgan, John H., and Goering, Rachel. "Caring for Parents Who Have Lost an Infant." *Journal of Religion and Health* 17 (October 1978):290-98.

Moriarty, David M., ed. *The Loss of Loved Ones.* Springfield, Ill., Charles C. Thomas, 1967.

Moriarty, Irene. "Sudden Death: Pastoral Presence with the Bereaved." *Journal of Pastoral Counseling* 15 (Fall-Winter 1980):41-49.

Morris, Paul. *Widows and Their Families.* London: Routledge & Kegan Paul, 1958.

Murphey, Cecil. *Comforting Those Who Grieve.* Atlanta: John Knox Press, 1979.

Nicol, Thomas. "Mourning." In *Dictionary of the Bible*, 3:453-54. Edited by James Hastings. New York: Charles Scribner's Sons, 1909.

Oates, Wayne E. *Anxiety in Christian Experience.* Philadelphia: Westminster Press, 1955.

_____. *Pastoral Care and Counseling in Grief and Separation.* Philadelphia: Fortress Press, 1976.

_____. "Rituals of Grief." *Thesis Theological Cassettes* 12 (March 1980).

_____. *The Bible in Pastoral Care.* Philadelphia: Westminster Press, 1953.

Organ, Troy. "Grief and the Art of Consolation." *The Christian Century* 96 (August 1979):759-62.

Parkes, Colin M. *Bereavement.* New York: International Universities Press, 1972.

Peretz, David. "Reaction to Loss." In *Loss and Grief: Psychological Management in Medical Practice,* pp. 20-35. Edited by Bernard Schoenberg, Arthur C. Carr, David Peretz, and Austin H. Kutscher. New York: Columbia University Press, 1970.

Pollock, George H. "Mourning and Adaptation." *International Journal of Psycho-Analysis* 42 (1961):346-55.

Redden, Jack. "An Evaluation of the Responses of Treated and Untreated Widows to Questions Presented Before and Following Group Treatment." M.A.R. guided research paper, Harding Graduate School of Religion, 1978.

Reed, Elizabeth L. *Helping Children with the Mystery of Death.* Nashville: Abingdon Press, 1970.

Rees, W. Dewi. "The Bereaved and Their Hallucinations." In *Bereavement: Its Psychosocial Aspects,* pp. 66-71. Edited by Bernard Schoenberg. New York: Columbia University Press, 1975.

Rogers, William F. "Needs of the Bereaved." *Pastoral Psychology* 1 (June 1950):17-21.

_____. "The Pastor's Work with Grief." *Pastoral Psychology* 14 (September 1963):22-27.

Roth, Cecil. "Aninut." In *Encyclopedia Judaica*, 3:23. Edited by Cecil Roth. Jerusalem: Keter Publishing House, 1971.

Schiff, Harriet S. *The Bereaved Parent.* New York: Crown Publishers, 1977.

Schneider, John. *Stress, Loss and Grief.* Baltimore: University Park Press, 1984.

Schoenberg, B. Mark. "When a Friend Is in Mourning." In *Bereavement Counseling*, pp. 239-49. Edited by B. Mark Schoenberg. Westport, Conn.: Greenwood Press, 1980.

————, ed. *Bereavement Counseling.* Westport, Conn.: Greenwood Press, 1980.

Smith, Henry P. *A Critical and Exegetical Commentary on the Books of Samuel.* Edinburgh, Scotland: T. & T. Clark, 1894.

Sobel, David E. "Death and Dying." *American Journal of Nursing* 74 (January 1974):98-99.

Spiegel, Yorick. *The Grief Process.* Translated by Elsbeth Duke. Nashville: Abingdon Press, 1973.

————. *The Grief Process: Analysis and Counseling.* Translated by Elsbeth Duke. Nashville: Abingdon Press, 1977.

Stone, Harold W. *Crisis Counseling.* Philadelphia: Fortress Press, 1976.

————. *Suicide and Grief.* Philadelphia: Fortress Press, 1972.

Sullender, R. Scott. "Three Theoretical Approaches to Grief." *The Journal of Pastoral Care* 33 (December 1979):243-51.

Switzer, David K. *The Minister as Crisis Counselor.* Nashville: Abindgon Press, 1974.

Tatelbaum, Judy. *The Courage to Grieve.* New York: Lippincott & Crowell Publishers, 1980.

Bibliography

Topolewshi, John L. "Death in the Family: A Model of Ministry." *Draw Gateway* 47 (1976-77):78-79.

Van Heukelem, Judith F. "Weep with Those Who Weep: Understanding and Helping the Crying Person." *Journal of Psychology and Theology* 7 (Summer 1979):83-91.

Van Meter, Mary Jane S., and White, Ronald K. "The Death Crisis and Pastoral Counseling." *Journal of Religion and Health* 21 (Fall 1982):235-44.

Volkan, Vamik. "Typical Findings in Pathological Grief." *Psychiatric Quartely* 44 (1970):231-350.

Westberg, Granger E. *Good Grief.* Philadelphia: Fortress Press, 1962.

——————. *Minister and Doctor Meet.* New York: Harper & Row, Publishers, 1961.

Wiehe, Verner R. "The Role of the Clergyman in the Grief Process." *Concordia Theological Monthly* 43 (March 1972):131-37.

Weiner, Alfred. "General Aspects." In *Understanding Bereavement and Grief*, pp. 37-44. Edited by Norman Linzer. New York: Yeshiva University Press, 1977.

Willis, R. Wayne. "Some Concerns of Bereaved Parents." *Journal of Religion and Health* 20 (Summer 1980): 133-40.

Wuthnow, Robert; Christiano, Kevin; and Kuzlowski, John. "Religion and Bereavement: A Conceptual Framework." *Journal for the Scientific Study of Religion* 19 (December 1980):408-22.

Zimbardo, Philip G. *Psychology and Life.* 9th ed. Glenview, Ill.: Scott, Foresman & Co., 1975.

NOTES

Chapter 1
1. Erich Lindemann, 'Symptomatology and Management of Acute Grief," in *Crisis Intervention*, ed. Howard J. Parad (New York: Family Service Association of America, 1965), 4.

Chapter 3
1. R. Scott Sullender, 'Three Theoretical Approaches to Grief," *Journal of Pastoral Care* 33 (December 1979): 251
2. Bill W. Flatt, *Mental Health and the Bible* (Memphis: Christian Counseling Publications, 1979), 69.
3. W. Dewi Rees, "The Bereaved and Their Hallucinations," in *Bereavement: Its Psychosocial Aspects*, ed. Bernard Schoenberg (New York: Columbia University Press, 1975), 67.

Chapter 4
1. Manfred H. Hecht, "Dynamics of Bereavement," *Journal of Religion and Health* 10 (October 1971): 361-62.

Chapter 5
1. Arthur Freese, *Help for Your Grief* (New York: Schocken Books, 1977), 60.
2. William S. Coffin, "Death: More Friend Than Foe," *The Christian Ministry* 16 (May 1985):6.
3. Eda LeShan, *Learning to Say Good-by* (New York: Hawthorn Books, 1976), 39.
4. Irene Moriarty, "Sudden Death: Pastoral Presence with the Bereaved," *Journal of Pastoral Counseling* 15 (Fall-Winter 1980):49.

Notes

Chapter 6

1. William Rogers, "Needs of the Bereaved," *Pastoral Psychology* 1 (June 1950):17-21.

2. Elizabeth N. Dixon, "When Birth Means Death," *Christian Ministry* 15 (July 1984):17.

3. William D. Alexy, "Dimensions of Psychological Counseling That Facilitate the Grieving Process of Bereaved Parents," *Journal of Counseling Psychology* 29 (September 1982):499.

4. Vamik Volkan, "Typical Findings in Pathological Grief," *Psychiatry Quarterly* 44 (1970):231-33.

5. Augustine, *The Confessions of St. Augustine,* trans. John K. Ryan (Garden City, N.Y.: Doubleday & Co., 1960), 98.

6. Lindemann, "Symptomatology," *Crisis Intervention,* 14-16.

Seminars and Lectures by Dr. Bill Flatt

This book will probably cause you to want to know more! Dr. Flatt, a minister, professor of counseling, and counseling psychologist, has conducted grief therapy groups and seminars for some 12 years and has studied extensively in this area. He has also spoken extensively on Mental Health and the Bible and on Building Better Families. Other books he has authored include *Since You Asked*, a question and answer book on the family and mental health; *Counseling Homosexuals*, and *From Worry to Happiness* all of which may be ordered from the Gospel Advocate Company.

In summary, Dr. Flatt could help you further:

1. By conducting a one-day workshop on Growing Through Grief.
2. By assisting you in starting a grief therapy support group.
3. By holding a weekend seminar on Mental Health and the Bible.
4. By holding a weekend meeting on Building Better Homes.
5. By supplying you with additional reading materials.

If you want to learn more, contact Dr. Flatt, at:

1226 Fair Meadow
Memphis, Tennessee 38117
901-682-5511